The History of the World According to facebook

Revised Edition

The History of the World

According to facebook

Revised Edition

Wylie Overstreet (author)

For information address HarperCollins Publishers, 195 Broadway, New York, NY 10007.

HarperCollins books may be purchased for educational, business, or sales promotional use. For information please email the Special Markets Department at SPsales@harpercollins.com.

A paperback edition of this book was published in 2011 by It Books, an imprint of HarperCollins Publishers.

FIRST DEY STREET PAPERBACK EDITION PUBLISHED 2018.

Designed by Timothy Shaner, nightanddaydesign.biz

Library of Congress Cataloging-in-Publication Data has been applied for.

ISBN 978-0-06-286908-1

18 19 20 21 22 LSC/ID 10 9 8 7 6 5 4 3 2 1

For my parents.

We Can Do It!
VOTES FOR WOMEN
#1
DVD
VIDEO
ENRON
HOLLYWOO
SEARS
GOD
CHICAGO
CUBS
MTV
bp
MADE IN CHINA
The New York Times
I ♥ NY
UNITED STATES ENVIRONMENTAL PROTECTION AGENCY
SKYNET

Introduction

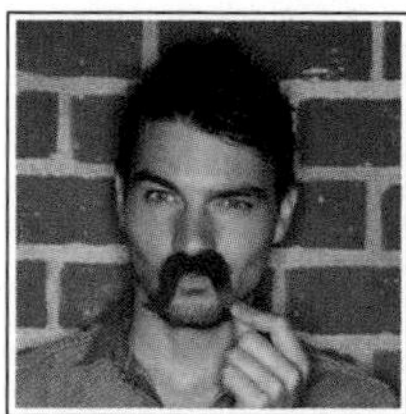

Ah, Facebook. We all make fun of it, and we're all on it. If the Facebook community—600 million strong—were a country, it would rank third in population and last in spelling ability. Nowadays Facebook is visited more often than Google, presumably because Google isn't as robust of a digital stalking tool.

But Facebook has only been around since 2004. In the grand scheme of things, this is not very long; in the time since, we've seen wars begin and end, revolutions succeed and fail, Lady Gaga wear a dress made of bacon, and this author go from madly in love to dumped and despondent, though he's not bitter. Tali. You bitch.

But the universe has been around for 13 billion years or, if you like reading fantasy novels, 12,000. What if Facebook had been around to record it all on that adorable little news feed? The dawn of time, of life, of man and civilization, of all our fits and starts, wars and squabbles, achievements and failures? What if Galileo was a tagging fiend, if Hitler liked his own statuses, if Patton checked in across North Africa posting pictures to make everyone envy how awesome his summer was going? Historians would probably sigh deeply, pour themselves a double, and mutter something about a "literary perversion" or "no respect for the field," or unrelatedly "where the hell are my goddamn keys."

Let's let them drink and look for their belongings and/or a better career while we take a look at the annals of history according to Facebook—from its first moments all those years ago to the present day. I sincerely hope you enjoy this book. You may find it educational, you may find it amusing, or you may find it on the back of a toilet while pooping, in which case you're not going anywhere for a while. Might as well flip through.

Again, enjoy.

And wash your hands.

The Singularity FIRST!!1!
13 billion years ago • Comment • Like

The Singularity Only one here. Right.
13 billion years ago • Like

The Singularity Phenomenal cosmic power, itty-bitty living space.
13 billion years ago • Comment • Like

Genie wurd.
13 billion years ago • Like

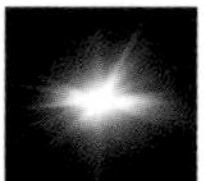

The Singularity is in a relationship with **Space** and **Time**, and it's complicated.
13 billion years ago • Comment • Like

Laws of Physics Really complicated.
13 billion years ago • Like

The Singularity

Singularity to Host "Big Bang" Cosmic Inauguration
All Matter in Universe Attending, Even Creationists

13 billion years ago • Comment • Like

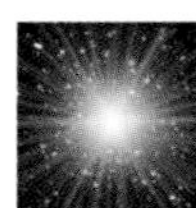

The Big Bang such a great party, thanks for everything that came.
13 billion years ago • Comment • Like

Dark Matter Just got here! Did I miss it?
13 billion years ago • Like

The Big Bang Yeah, sorry. It only lasted 3 trillionths of a second.
13 billion years ago • Like

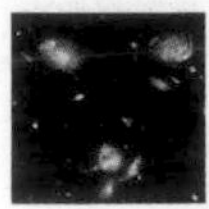

The Universe pics from my birthday party

13 billion years ago • Comment • Like

Carl Sagan likes this.

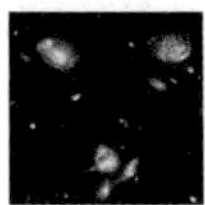

The Universe is now married to **Entropy.**

13 billion years ago • Comment • Like

The Second Law of Thermodynamics Watch out, she'll drain you. Trust me.

13 billion years ago • Like

Gravity > Nebula Ya got talent, kid, I'll give ya that. With my help you could even be famous... be a somebody, ya know? You watch, stick with me kiddo and I'll make ya a star!

13 billion years ago • Comment • Like

Fusion likes this.

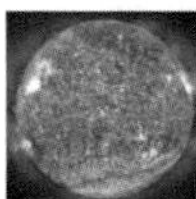

The Sun is now friends with **Earth** and **7 other planets.**

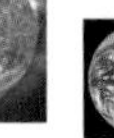
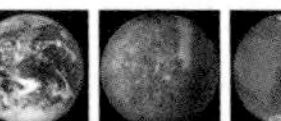
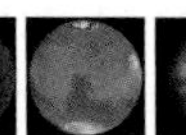

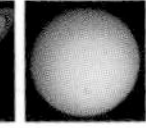

13 billion years ago • Comment • Like

Pluto Not cool.

13 billion years ago • Like

Uranus For the last time, the accent is on my FIRST syllable.
13 billion years ago • Comment • Like

Mercury I hear you're full of gas.
13 billion years ago • Like

Jupiter lol
13 billion years ago • Like

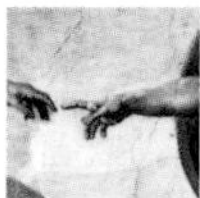

God Okey doke, time to make some shit. Starting with the Heavens and Earth.
13 billion years ago • Comment • Like

God Wait, I can't see a thing. I wonder if I can maybe...
13 billion years ago • Like

God Ah! Let there be it!

Light

13 billion years ago • Comment • Like

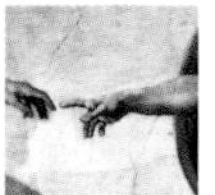

God tagged the **Heavens** and the **Earth** in his own album.

The Beginning

13 billion years ago • Comment • Like

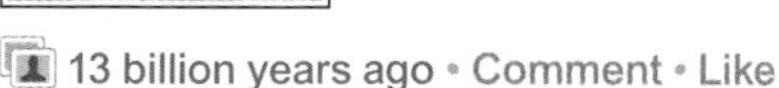

Earth is in a domestic partnership with the **Moon**.
13 billion years ago • Comment • Like

Tides like this.

The Moon added **Werewolves** to its Interests.
13 billion years ago • Comment • Like

Vampires Dislike.
13 billion years ago • Like

The Moon added **Menstrual Cycles** to its Interests.
13 billion years ago • Comment • Like

Vampires Like!
13 billion years ago • Like

The Moon That time of the month.

13 billion years ago • Comment • Like

Werewolf Oh no not agaAARGH
13 billion years ago • Like

Earth Delish!

Primordial Soup
If you have a few extra amino acids and organic compounds lying around, you might try making this unqiue...

13 billion years ago • Comment • Like

Earth > Life Listen, I have a feeling you're going to be the next big thing. You gotta start thinking about merchandising your brand name. Maybe a breakfast cereal and a board game, you know?
13 billion years ago • Comment • Like

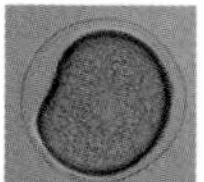

Single-Celled Organism is in a relationship with itself.
13 billion years ago • Comment • Like

Earth ??
13 billion years ago • Like

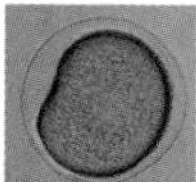

It's complicated between **Single-Celled Organism** and itself.
13 billion years ago • Comment • Like

Earth wtf?
13 billion years ago • Like

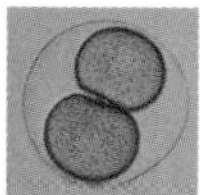

Single-Celled Organism is separated from itself.
13 billion years ago • Comment • Like

Mitosis likes this.

Earth Ooooooh. Got it. Nice.
13 billion years ago • Like

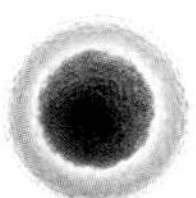

Life is in a relationship with **Evolution**.
13 billion years ago • Comment • Like

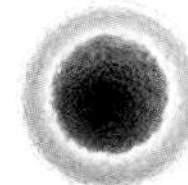

Life added **Photosynthesis** to its Interests.
13 billion years ago • Comment • Like

The Sun Mooch.
13 billion years ago • Like

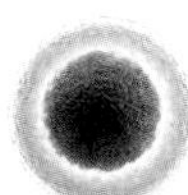

Life Not sure if I can survive on land.
13 billion years ago • Comment • Like

Dr. Ian Malcolm Pretty sure that, that, uh, you will, uh... find a way.
13 billion years ago • Like

Evolution I got your back.
13 billion years ago • Like

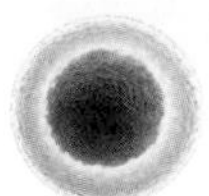

Life created an event.

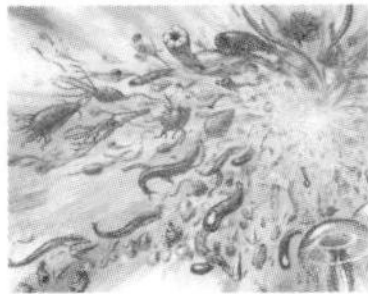

Cambrian Explosion
Single-Cell is so last millennium! Come ring in Multi-Cell and get all mutated!

13 billion years ago • Comment • Like • Share • RSVP to this event

Evolution Can't wait. I'm gonna get drunk and go bonkers.
13 billion years ago • Like

Earth is now friends with **Flora** and **Fauna**.

13 billion years ago • Comment • Like

Tyrannosaurus Rex

13 billion years ago • Comment • Like

Stegosaurus Badass pic, Rex. Except what's up with your arms?
13 billion years ago • Like

Evolution My mistake. They seemed to make sense at the time.
13 billion years ago • Like

Velociraptor added **Problem Solving** to its Interests.
13 billion years ago • Comment • Like

Earth Clever girl.
13 billion years ago • Like

Asteroid Hitting up Earth today, if ya know what I mean.
13 billion years ago • Comment • Like

Tyrannosaurus Rex Noooooooo
13 billion years ago • Like

Stegosaurus Noooooooo
13 billion years ago • Like

Brontosaurus Noooooooo
13 billion years ago • Like

Earth fml
13 billion years ago • Like

Cockroach lol
13 billion years ago • Like

Mammals > Dinosaurs Na na na naa, hey hey hey... goodbye.

Dinosaurs Extinct
Warm-Blooded Wombed Furballs Take Over Planet

 13 billion years ago • Comment • Like

---

Primates check out my new opposable thumbs

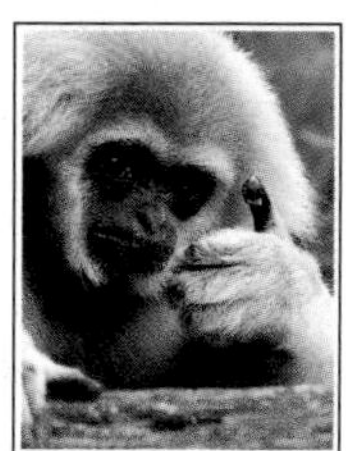

13 billion years ago • Comment • Like

Lobster Whoa, weird. What do you use them for?
13 billion years ago • Like

Primates All kinds of things: gripping branches, picking out lice, masturbating, etc.
13 billion years ago • Like

Lobster What is "masturbating"?
13 billion years ago • Like

Primates The BEST.
13 billion years ago • Like

Neanderthal Why doesn't the glowing heat orb just STAY in the sky?!
300,000 years ago • Comment • Like

Homo Erectus ooo, just discovered this!

300,000 years ago • Comment • Like

Homo Erectus warm warm warm warm!

300,000 years ago • Comment • Like

Homo Erectus HOT HOT BURN BURN!

300,000 years ago • Comment • Like

Dawn of Man

After brutal eons of natural selection, evolution managed to iron out the wrinkles of a certain branch of apes and produce a hairless smarty-pants upgrade: us.

Modern science has removed all doubt from Mr. Darwin's theory. Our ancestors were primates—with whom we still share DNA—and long ago we came down from the trees, began walking upright, and evolved a higher intelligence. We started making tools and using fire. We began speaking to each other. If something made us angry, we used language to communicate instead of just shrieking loudly like our tree-dwelling ancestors—or the creationists currently reading this.

Emerging from Africa, our species flourished across the continents. We used our smarts to invent the wheel, agriculture, cargo pants, and Bud Light Lime. Our civilizations spread like the wings of chicken held upside down, proving that we were the planet's dominant species and that analogies are not my strong suit.

The evolution of man was not a perfect process (foreskin? really?), but the emergence of man began an epoch of dominance that will continue in perpetuity, or until we fuck it up.

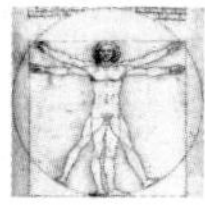

Homo Sapiens Good news! My brain is huge.
300,000 years ago • Comment • Like

Neanderthal And I just saved a ton of money on my car insurance.
300,000 years ago • Like

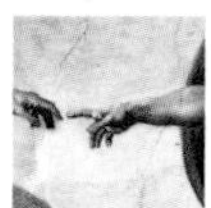

God Accidentally sneezed on a pile of dust and now there's a naked dude standing in my foyer. You gotta be careful with this omnipotence thing.
300,000 years ago • Comment • Like

Adam
Nice, but kinda lonely — is in **Eden**.
300,000 years ago • Comment • Like

Adam Anyone know what long-term complications can arise from a missing rib?
300,000 years ago • Comment • Like

God Pipe down, you'll like what I'm making.
300,000 years ago • Like

Adam is now friends with **Eve**.

300,000 years ago • Comment • Like

Eve likes **Paradise**.
300,000 years ago • Comment • Like

God Who doesn't, amiright?
300,000 years ago • Like

Eve was tagged in **Snake**'s photo.

300,000 years ago • Comment • Like

Snake Make you hungry for one?
300,000 years ago • Like

Eve Yeah, but this bikini bod isn't gonna keep itself thin.
300,000 years ago • Like

Snake created an event.

Fruit Tasting!
Organic, locally grown and sustainably farmed!

31 300,000 years ago • Comment • Like • Share • RSVP to this event

Eve Sorry, I'm on a master cleanse!
300,000 years ago • Like

Snake This is harder than I thought.
300,000 years ago • Like

Eve What is?
300,000 years ago • Like

Snake Nothing, forget it.
300,000 years ago • Like

Snake > **Eve**

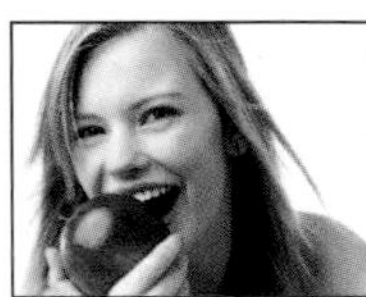
Study Reveals "Knowledge Apple" Benefits
Slimmer Figure, Clear Skin, Only One Tiny Caveat

300,000 years ago • Comment • Like

Eve omg rly?!
300,000 years ago • Like

Snake Who knew, right?
300,000 years ago • Like

Eve Wait, what's a "caveat"?
300,000 years ago • Like

Snake Uh... 10 calories.
300,000 years ago • Like

Eve omg really? I guess I could use a snack...
300,000 years ago • Like

Adam NO STOP
300,000 years ago • Like

God > Eve Fail.
300,000 years ago • Comment • Like

Eve was tagged in **God's** album.

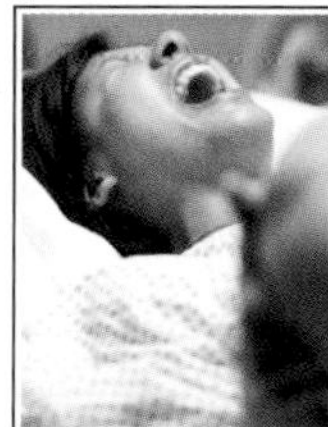

Childbirth

300,000 years ago • Comment • Like

Adam Ooooo, sucky.
300,000 years ago • Like

Akhmed Just invented a way to record language.

Cuneiform Script

30,000 BC • Comment • Like

Nemenhat Whoa. What's it say?
30,000 BC • Like

Akhmed "Steve owes me a goat."
30,000 BC • Like

Nemenhat That's all? Seems like there should be more.
30,000 BC • Like

Steve Bullshit, I owe you a chicken.
30,000 BC • Like

Akhmed It also says "Steve is a cheap bastard."
30,000 BC • Like

The Ice Age is now friends with **Earth**.

30,000 BC • Comment • Like

Glaciers like this.

Mayans Sure, we may be dying out, but at least we're aren't those poor suckers who have to be around when it hits the fan in the early 21st century.
30,000 BC • Comment • Like

Roland Emmerich likes this.

God As a token of my gratitude, I gave my boy **@Noah** a 5-day, 4-night cruise on the (very) high seas!
30,000 BC • Comment • Like

Noah Whaaaat! This is amazing, G! Thanks!
30,000 BC • Like

God No worries man, you deserve it. Small note--you gotta build the boat.
30,000 BC • Like

Noah Wait, what?
30,000 BC • Like

God And you have to take a breeding pair of every animal with you. So you probably should make it big.
30,000 BC • Like

Noah Whoa, hang on, I don't know about this.
30,000 BC • Like

God Aaaand there's a giant flood coming, so if you don't, you'll die.
30,000 BC • Like

Noah Dick.
30,000 BC • Like

God :-D
30,000 BC • Like

Noah posted a picture.

30,000 BC • Comment • Like

God Nice!
30,000 BC • Like

Noah So is the invoice, which is in the mail.
30,000 BC • Like

Noah — is in the **Ark** with a **Elephants**, **Turtles**, **Guinea Pigs**, and a **bajillion other animals**.
30,000 BC • Comment • Like

Noah Wow, smells... really great in here.
30,000 BC • Like

God Sarcasm doesn't get you into heaven.
30,000 BC • Like

Noah In hindsight putting the pigeons and jaguars together was a bad move. Also, anyone have any extra pigeons by any chance?
30,000 BC • Comment • Like

Noah > God How about letting those waters recede? It's been a couple days....
30,000 BC • Comment • Like

God Yeah, no prob. Send out a bird or something to look for land. You got any pigeons?
30,000 BC • Like

Noah Uh, does a dove work?
30,000 BC • Like

God Yeah, sure, whatever.
30,000 BC • Like

Dove

30,000 BC • Comment • Like

Noah Phew.
30,000 BC • Like

God Nice. When you die you can come hang with me by my infinity pool and drink mai tais. Hollaaaaa.
30,000 BC • Like

God > Abraham Big A, you still owe me ten bucks from minigolf last week.
1770 BC • Comment • Like

Abraham I don't get paid till next month.
1770 BC • Like

God Well then sacrifice your son to me.
1770 BC • Like

Isaac Uh, Dad? Why the knife?
1770 BC • Like

Abraham Sorry, kiddo. Hold still.
1770 BC • Like

God WHOA DUDE STOP
1770 BC • Like

Abraham But...
1770 BC • Like

God Sarcasm! Just give me cash whenever, sheesh.
1770 BC • Like

Abraham Oh. Sorry, I can never tell.
1770 BC • Like

God Really? You think I'm the kind of guy who'd require the sacrifice of a beloved son?
1770 BC • Like

Jesus Christ ...
1770 BC • Like

God That was different.
1770 BC • Like

Isaac I hate u! Worst dad EVER!
1770 BC • Comment • Like

Abraham Oh relax. Write about it on your livejournal or something.
1770 BC • Like

Pharaoh Offering a great investment opportunity in a giant tomb construction project. Buy in early, then recruit others to maximize your returns! Message me for details.
1440 BC • Comment • Like

Ra likes this.

Worker Is this a pyramid scheme?
1440 BC • Like

Pharaoh Interesting you say that...
1440 BC • Like

Moses > Pharaoh Dude. My people. Let them go.
1440 BC • Comment • Like

God likes this.

Pharaoh Look, man, I totally get where you're coming from, but honestly good slave labor is hard to find these days. I gotta keep my eye on the bottom line here, especially with these "Pyramid" things in the works sooo yeah, sorry.
1440 BC • Like

Moses alright we're outta here
1440 BC • Like

Pharaoh is now friends with **Locusts**, **Frogs**, and **8 other plagues**.

  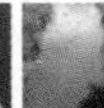 

1440 BC • Comment • Like

Moses and The Israelites like this.

Pharaoh Alright, GTFO
1440 BC • Like

Moses Outta here. Parting the Red Sea....

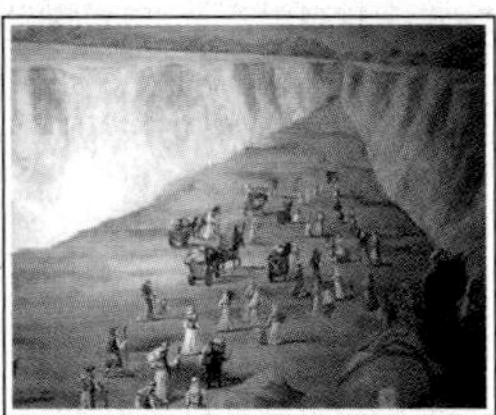

1440 BC • Comment • Like

Egyptian Soldier :-O
1440 BC • Like

Moses ...aaand closing the Red Sea.
1440 BC • Comment • Like

Egyptian Soldier wtf is this magic
1440 BC • Like

Egyptian Soldier oh no here comes the wat
1440 BC • Like

The Israelites lol
1440 BC • Like

God Sly move, M! Side note--got a pair of stone tablets I'd love for you to take a look at. Hit me on the cellie.
1440 BC • Like

Moses > God "Thou shalt not thank me during post-game interviews"?
1440 BC • Comment • Like

God What, I find it insincere.
1440 BC • Like

Moses We're taking that one off. 10 is a nice round number anyway.
1440 BC • Like

God Fine.
1440 BC • Like

Helen of Sparta — is in **Troy**.
1184 BC • Comment • Like

Paris likes this.

Menelaus thought we were wine tasting today, babe
1184 BC • Like

Helen of Troy changed her current city to **Troy**.
1184 BC • Comment • Like

Menelaus Did your acct. get hacked babe?
1184 BC • Like

Paris If that's what they're calling it these days, then yea lol
1184 BC • Like

Helen of Sparta is in a relationship with **Paris.**
1184 BC • Comment • Like

Menelaus That's it, I'm coming after you, pretty boy.
1184 BC • Like

Paris haha, you and what army?
1184 BC • Like

Agamemnon Mine.
1184 BC • Like

Paris O_o
1184 BC • Like

King Priam FML
1184 BC • Like

Agamemnon A thousand should do it.

1184 BC • Comment • Like

Achilles > Odysseus Hey man, did I leave my ankle armor in your chariot?
1184 BC • Comment • Like

Paris like this.

Trojan Army Victory! 10 years of siege and we've finally driven off the Gree... whoa. Wait a tick. Did someone misplace a giant wooden horsey thing?
1184 BC • Comment • Like

Odysseus Oh, dang! Yeah, that's ours... must've left it behind by purpose.
1184 BC • Like

Odysseus Er, by accident. Anyway, it's all yours. Might look good inside the city walls next to like a fountain or a pillar or something. Anywhere inside the city walls, really.
1184 BC • Like

Trojan Army Wow, thanks fellas.
1184 BC • Like

Greek Army Oh of course, it's our city.
1184 BC • Like

Greek Army Er, our pleasure.
1184 BC • Like

Penelope long and winding rooooooad

Motley Crue "Home Sweet Home"

1184 BC • Comment • Like

Odysseus On my way!
1184 BC • Like

Suitors shit.
1184 BC • Like

Syrens > Odysseus Hey babe, wanna stop by our island? Promise to make it worth your while ;-)
1184 BC • Comment • Like

Odysseus I want to go to there.
1184 BC • Like

Syrens Just park your boat on the rocks.
1184 BC • Like

Syrens I mean the beach.
1184 BC • Like

Odysseus My shipmates are cockblocks and refusing to go. My hands are tied. :-(
1184 BC • Like

Syrens You're the captain, though!
1184 BC • Like

Odysseus No, I mean my hands are literally tied to the mast. Actually, this may have been my idea.
1184 BC • Like

Goliath I swear, you have one off day and everybody hates you. I'm going to go sit in the shower until the hot water runs out.
1020 BC • Comment • Like

David likes this.

Jonah is now friends with **The Whale**.

765 BC • Comment • Like

Jonah Can't see a thing in here. And it smells like low tide.
765 BC • Like

Oedipus is in a relationship with **Queen Jocasta**.
492 BC • Comment • Like

Queen Jocasta likes this.

Creon She's a bit older, no?
492 BC • Like

Sappho OMG so happy for you! You guys look great together! And a little alike, actually.
492 BC • Like

Oracle of Delphi She's your mom, dude.
492 BC • Like

Creon LOL JER-RY JER-RY JER-RY!
492 BC • Like

Socrates Got stopped and given a ticket for "corrupting the youth."
399 BC • Comment • Like

👍 **Bill and Ted like this.**

Plato Ouch. What's the fine?
399 BC • Like

Socrates Hm. Not so bad, it just says I have to drink hemlock.
399 BC • Like

Plato ...
399 BC • Like

Aristotle ...
399 BC • Like

Socrates What?
399 BC • Like

Plato Hemlock is lethal.
399 BC • Like

Socrates This day just keeps getting better.
399 BC • Like

Socrates > Greek Magistrates For what it's worth, you guys gotta come up with a better way to do this. This hemlock stuff tastes like cut grass. Though it seems to work qui
399 BC • Comment • Like

Alexander the Great — is in **Greece** with the **Macedonian Army.**
330 BC • Comment • Like

Alexander the Great — is in **Persia** with the **Macedonian Army.**
330 BC • Comment • Like

Alexander the Great — is in **Egypt** with the **Macedonian Army.**
330 BC • Comment • Like

Alexander the Great — is in **Arabia** with the **Macedonian Army.**
330 BC • Comment • Like

Alexander the Great — is in **Mesopotamia** with the **Macedonian Army.**
330 BC • Comment • Like

Alexander the Great — is in **India** with the **Macedonian Army.**
330 BC • Comment • Like

Macedonian Army You know, we could use a break.
330 BC • Like

Marcus Aurelius Coliseum Madness! Fill out your bracket, winner takes all.
172 BC • Comment • Like

Gladiator Am I on the schedule?
172 BC • Like

Marcus Aurelius Yep! You'll be fighting a tiger.
172 BC • Like

Gladiator I'm sorry?
172 BC • Like

Marcus Aurelius A tiger. Orange cat... stripes...
172 BC • Like

Gladiator I know what a tiger is. I would rather not fight one, as they tend to be furry balls of murder.
172 BC • Like

Gladiator tagged **Marcus Aurelius** in his album.

Are You Not Entertained!?

172 BC • Comment • Like

Oracle > Julius Caesar Had a dream with you in it last night and woke up feeling like I should warn you of... something. Having a hard time recalling it though. Something about March... "The Tides of March" maybe? Ring any bells?
44 BC • Comment • Like

Julius Caesar Nope. Let's not hope it's not life or death.
44 BC • Like

Cleopatra added **Eyeliner** to her Interests.
44 BC • Comment • Like

Marc Antony and **Julius Caesar** like this.

Julius Caesar having a few of the fellas over to the palace tonight for a killer party.
44 BC • Comment • Like

Brutus Oh it's gonna be killer alright.
44 BC • Like

Julius Caesar hahah dude don't be creepy.
44 BC • Like

Age of Wonder

As humanity progressed, we began to question things beyond our immediate understanding. Where did we come from? Why are we here? Who exactly let the dogs out? We dipped our toe into the cold, dark waters of the existential, shivered, and found religion.

God became our guiding light in the darkness of the unknown. We found meaning in His words, comfort in His promise, and a great reason to kill each other in His name. Empirical evidence of his existence remains elusive. Luckily, with humans, the absence of fact is rarely a hindrance. Actually it might get you a show on Fox News.

In the Western world, Christianity became the dominant faith. If you're unfamiliar with Christianity, you're either a remarkably sheltered individual or a member of a malicious alien race who found this book among the ruins of our now-conquered civilization, in which case, welcome, congratulations on your new planet, check out the south of France in the spring. It's lovely.

Today, Christianity offers humans the same basic comforts and purpose it did when we first invent—er, discovered it. It's a chance at salvation and eternal bliss in the embrace of a deity who loves you just the way you are. Unless you are gay.

Mary OMFG. I'm pregnant.
0 BC • Comment • Like

Joseph Uh you're a virgin, babe. I should know lol
0 BC • Like

God "OMFG" is right!
0 BC • Like

Joseph Wait...
0 BC • Like

Joseph Oh not cool.
0 BC • Like

Holy Ghost lol someone call Maury.
0 BC • Like

John the Apostle — is at the **Marriage at Cana** with **Jesus** and **11 others**.
30 • Comment • Like

John the Apostle Crashing wedding with bunch of friends? $0. Watching J pull his water-into-wine party trick? $0. Everyone's reaction? Priceless.
30 • Like

Peter the Apostle John, come meet us out back by the fire pit. Paul is tanked and singing "Your Body Is a Wonderland" to the bridesmaids.
30 • Like

Jesus > Peter the Apostle dude what happened last night?!
30 • Comment • Like

Peter the Apostle It got a little crazy, man. Put it this way, we should probably ease up on the partying for a while, and we should definitely not go back to that temple for a looong time.
30 • Like

Jesus invited you to **The Last Supper.**
30 • Comment • Like

Peter the Apostle "Last"?
30 • Like

Jesus Long story, but let's just say you guys need to buck up on your loyalty.
30 • Like

Judas Iscariot > Jesus Swing by tonight, having a little garden party.
30 • Comment • Like

Pontius Pilate likes this.

Jesus Isn't it a little chilly for that?
30 • Like

Judas Iscariot Um, yeah. Winter.
30 • Like

Jesus was tagged in **Judas Iscariot**'s photo.

Kisses!

30 • Comment • Like

Roman Soldiers Thanks.
30 • Like

Jesus Christ oh balls.
30 • Like

God created an event.

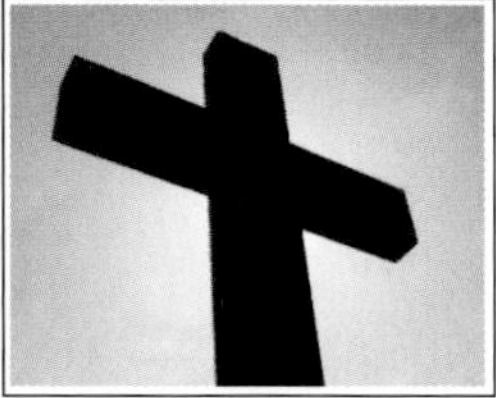

Crucifixion Party!
Wear a funny hat, a crown of thorns, or a cool loincloth!

31 30 • Comment • Like • Share • RSVP to this event

God RSVPed for you, J.
30 • Like

Jesus You owe me for this.
30 • Like

Jesus is in **The Cave.**
30 • Comment • Like

Peter the Apostle I'm going to come by and pay my respects.
30 • Like

Jesus Well be quick about it, I'm only here for another 2 days.
30 • Like

Peter the Apostle wha?!
30 • Like

Peter the Apostle > **Judas Iscariot** Dude, what were you thinking?
30 • Comment • Like

Satan likes this.

Judas Iscariot Sorry, but he sayeth-ed unto me one too many times. And whenever I asked him for rent, he'd give me some parable about sowing seeds on stony ground. What does that even mean!? Besides, I owed my cousin Carl thirty pieces of silver.
30 • Like

Peter the Apostle Wow. So you don't care who his dad is?
30 • Like

Judas Iscariot His dad?
30 • Like

Peter the Apostle Starts with a G...
30 • Like

Judas Iscariot Oh fuck.
30 • Like

Zeus > God You gotta let me know how you manage to get heaps of praise and devotion while I'm over here getting offered charred livestock carcasses. These things smell TERRIBLE.
30 • Comment • Like

Athena likes this.

Hades Yeah man, it's looking like a damn petting zoo down here with all the new goat souls.
30 • Like

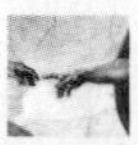

God You gotta have your only child go down there and get crucified.
30 • Like

Jesus Christ Which totally sucks, btw.
30 • Like

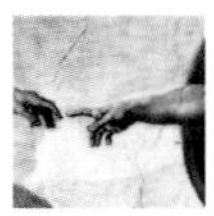

God Wonder what this button does....
79 • Comment • Like

Pompeii AHHHHH IT BURNS
79 • Like

God Oh wow. My bad.
79 • Like

Vesuvius LOL
79 • Like

The Dark Ages is friends with **Leprosy, Gout,** and **6 other diseases.**

425 • Comment • Like

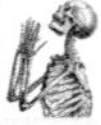

The Dark Ages Coming to the realization that nothing all that cool happened during my lifetime.
425 • Comment • Like

The Dark Ages There were some pretty gruesome battles I guess. Though that's not exactly all sunshine and rainbows.
590 • Comment • Like

The Dark Ages Oh, and the plague. I had lots of plague. Not fun.
635 • Comment • Like

Bubonic Plague Whaaat! Dude, we had a blast!
635 • Like

Peasants A bunch of us starved too.
635 • Like

The Dark Ages Again, not exactly a good thing.
635 • Like

The Dark Ages What about the death of the Roman Empire? Does that qualify as important? Still not uplifting, but I'll take important.
770 • Comment • Like

The Dark Ages In retrospect, my time was just composed of lots of people dying.
810 • Comment • Like

Industrial Revolution Who are you talking to?
810 • Like

The Dark Ages Shut up man, you're not even around for another couple centuries.
810 • Like

Renaissance

The Renaissance was a time of profound intellectual, scientific, and artistic growth. After the Dark Ages, centuries over which humanity made great strides in the perfection of starving and dying, the Renaissance was a period of rebirth. It was the age of legendary painters like Leonardo and Raphael as well as sculptors like Michelangelo and Donatello, all of whom valiantly fought the Foot Clan.

Artists were always completing new work, so long as their subject was religious. Scientists were always finding new truths, much to the chagrin of the religious. Yes, the Renaissance gave us innumerable artistic masterpieces, new knowledge about the universe, and many centuries later a type of "Faire" attended by eccentric white folks in costume.

With the exception of Shakespeare, who was OK, I guess, the Renaissance was centered in Italy. We're not sure what they were putting in the water back then, but considering the creative genius it produced, we're hoping Hollywood rips a few lines of it before Adam Sandler has a chance to release another movie.

Renaissance > The Dark Ages Yooo, what up homie! Sorry I'm late, but hey, party doesn't start till I arrrOOH daaaaaamn. What is that smell?! Dude what happened here? This place is a mess.

1045 • Comment • Like

The Dark Ages -sigh- There was a lot of disease and death.

1045 • Like

Renaissance I get that, the odors make my eyes water.

1045 • Like

Ice Age Don't be too hard on yourself, D. All I did was kill things off.

1045 • Like

Renaissance alright enough with the pity party, who wants to paint a ceiling or invent some shit?

1045 • Like

The Pope Anyone up for starting a war? Or some witch hunting? Honestly I'm just bored.

1187 • Comment • Like

Peasant Joe How about an uplifting sermon for your followers?

1187 • Like

The Pope Oh yah that sound great let's do that insteaZZZZzzzzzz. C'mon.

1187 • Like

The Pope added **Pointy Hats** to his Interests.

1187 • Comment • Like

The Pope We're out of burning stakes, so I guess I'm conquering the Holy Land.

1187 • Comment • Like

Muslims Our Holy Land?

1187 • Like

The Pope not for long, lol
1187 • Like

Muslims Have you ever been here? It's a barren desert.
1187 • Like

The Pope sure, but it's a HOLY dessert.
1187 • Like

Muslims Desert.
1187 • Like

The Pope whatevs
1187 • Like

Muslim You know that little hat of yours looks awfully a lot like a dunce cap.
1187 • Like

The Pope What's that?
1187 • Like

Muslims Wow, is it?
1187 • Like

The Pope > Richard the Lionheart Broski, this weekend--u, me, ur army, the Holy Land. Boom. Gonna be off the hook.
1187 • Comment • Like

Richard the Lionheart What Holy Land? Jerusalem?
1187 • Like

The Pope Yup, and actually it'd just be u, ur army, and the Holy Land. I gotta stay here and do... stuff.
1187 • Like

Richard the Lionheart Why would we want to conquer a barren desert?
1187 • Like

The Pope What part of "HOLY" don't u understand?
1187 • Like

The Pope created an event.

The Crusades
Cuz Their Holy Stuff
Should be Our Holy Stuff

31 1187 • Comment • Like • Share • RSVP to this event

Richard the Lionheart How am I listed as attending? I never responded to this.
1187 • Like

The Pope Made u an admin. U gotta come.
1187 • Like

Richard the Lionheart changed **The Crusades** to **Pointless Religious Conflict**.
31 1187 • Comment • Like

The Pope u ASS
1187 • Like

The Pope changed **Pointless Religious Conflict** to **The Crusades**.
31 1187 • Comment • Like

Richard the Lionheart You know what that hat of yours looks like?
1187 • Like

Richard the Lionheart — is in **Jerusalem** with **English Crusaders**.
1187 • Comment • Like

Richard the Lionheart And oh look, it's a barren desert. Shocker.
1187 • Like

The Pope that's it, ur not coming to the afterparty.
1187 • Like

Dante Alighieri Ugh, this is hell.
June 2, 1313 • Comment • Like

Brunetto Latini Oh no, what is?
June 2, 1313 • Like

Dante Alighieri This is.
June 2, 1313 • Like

Brunetto Latini Got that, but what's "hell" right now?
June 2, 1313 • Like

Dante Alighieri Here. Where I am.
June 2, 1313 • Like

Brunetto Latini Okaaaay... Where are you?
June 2, 1313 • Like

Dante Alighieri Hell.
June 2, 1313 • Like

Brunetto Latini I noticed. Jesus.
June 2, 1313 • Like

Dante Alighieri You did? Where? I don't think he's down here.
June 2, 1313 • Like

Brunetto Latini Oh my god. Just tell me where you are.
June 2, 1313 • Like

Dante Alighieri OK he's *definitely* not around here.
June 2, 1313 • Like

Brunetto Latini What the hell are you talking about?
June 2, 1313 • Like

Dante Alighieri Yes! Exactly.
June 2, 1313 • Like

Brunetto Latini GOD DAMMIT
June 2, 1313 • Like

Dante Alighieri He did! The whole place!
June 2, 1313 • Like

Satan > Dante Alighieri Great times hangin' with you and Virgil, dude. Hope to see you back here soon! Er, not like that.
June 2, 1313 • Comment • Like

Virgil likes this.

Robin Hood — is at **Sherwood Forest**.
1400 • Comment • Like

Sheriff of Nottingham CRIMINAL
1400 • Like

Robin Hood Just trying to spread the wealth around, Sheriff.
1400 • Like

Sheriff of Nottingham SOCIALIST
1400 • Like

Robin Hood is now married to **Maid Marian**.
1400 • Comment • Like

Robin Hood I'd fight for you. I'd lie for you. Walk the wire for you.
1400 • Like

Friar Tuck Barf.
1400 • Like

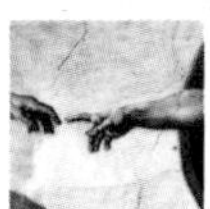

God > Joan of Arc Hey little lady. Just wanted to check in, see what's happening on your farm. From where I sit, I think you should lead the battle to free France.
1430 • Comment • Like

Joan of Arc As you wish, my lord. It shall be my destiny.
1430 • Like

God Oh wait, my phone autocorrected that. Meant to say "lead the cattle to free grass." Don't go joinin' the war, k?
1430 • Like

God OK, homegirl?
1430 • Like

God Joan? Hello?
1430 • Like

Joan of Arc is now friends with **Charles VII**.

1430 • Comment • Like

Joan of Arc — is at the **Siege of Orleans** with **Charles VII**.
1430 • Comment • Like

France likes this.

God Uh oh.
1430 • Like

Charles VII

Victory at the Siege of Orleans
Some "Joan" Girl Totally Kicked Ass

1430 • Comment • Like

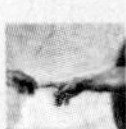
God Wow. Not expecting this.
1430 • Like

Joan of Arc > **Charles VII** Give me leadership of your entire army.
1430 • Comment • Like

Charles VII Uhhh...why?
1430 • Like

Joan of Arc God told me it was my destiny.
1430 • Like

God About that...
1430 • Like

Leonardo da Vinci Some new designs.

1430 • Comment • Like

Hudson Hawk and Dan Brown like this.

Joan of Arc

Victory at Patay
Joan of Arc Goes 2 for 2, Signs Endorsement Deal with Catholic Church

 1430 • Comment • Like

Charles VII GO SHAWTY
1430 • Like

God Holy crap.
1430 • Like

Joan of Arc — is in **Reims, France** with **Charles VII**.
1430 • Comment • Like

Charles VII Holllaaaaa, time to get coronated.
1430 • Like

God Look, this has been an impressive romp, but Joan, I really think you gotta ease up before your luck runs out...
1430 • Like

English Army Gotcha.
1430 • Like

God ...like that.
1430 • Like

Joan of Arc was tagged in **England**'s album.

LOL BBQ

1430 • Comment • Like

Joan of Arc I have listened to you, my Lord, and lived my life by your commands.

1430 • Like

God Mmm... kinda.

1430 • Like

Joan of Arc What?

1430 • Like

God Forget it, I'll explain in person. See you in a sec.

1430 • Like

Christopher Columbus LANDED! Amazing feeling to arrive in... wait does anyone know where we are?

1492 • Comment • Like

First Mate No idea, sir.

1492 • Like

Christopher Columbus Anyone care to make an educated guess?

1492 • Like

Christopher Columbus Anyone? Anyone? Bueller?

1492 • Like

Francisco Bueller Um... India?

1492 • Like

Christopher Columbus OK then! India. Hm. Well I guess we'll call these natives "Indians."

1492 • Like

Native Americans Let's hope that doesn't stick.
1492 • Like

Michelangelo Finished!

August 11, 1503 • Comment • Like

King David Hey dude, looks great except for one... tiny... thing.
August 11, 1503 • Like

Michelangelo What? Oooooh, right. Well I was just being true to the original.
August 11, 1503 • Like

King David Alright, wow, not helping. You couldn't have just gone with a fig leaf or a tastefully draped robe?
August 11, 1503 • Like

Michelangelo I really don't see the problem here.
August 11, 1503 • Like

Queen Bathsheba Lord knows I do.
August 11, 1503 • Like

Michelangelo lol
August 11, 1503 • Like

Leonardo da Vinci added a photo to his album.

Portrait by an Artist of a Young Woman

1510 • Comment • Like

Mona Lisa What's up with my smile?
1510 • Like

Leonardo da Vinci 16th-century dentistry, babe. Trust me.
1510 • Like

Martin Luther Anyone have a hammer I can borrow?
October 31, 1517 • Comment • Like

Hernan Cortes Just pulled up in the New World. Gonna take a nap, then off to conquer.
March 1519 • Comment • Like

Aztecs Whoa whoa whoa. This land is occupado, amigo. Also, there's like a hundred of you and a bazillion of us.
March 1519 • Like

Hernan Cortes You ever meet my friend Smallpox?
March 1519 • Like

Aztecs Smallwho?
March 1519 • Like

Hernan Cortes I'll introduce you.
March 1519 • Like

Henry the VIII Yay great, another daughter. #sarcasm
January 1536 • Comment • Like

Anne Boleyn Well I can't just will a boy into existence, honey. It's not up to me, so don't lose your head about it.
January 1536 • Like

Henry the VIII Oh I won't, *honey*. You might.
January 1536 • Like

Michelangelo Done. My arms are sooooooore.

1541 • Comment • Like

Raphael I'm happy for you, and I'ma let you finish, but Leonardo had one of the best frescos of all time. Of all time.

1541 • Like

Adam Wow, looks great except you apparently mistook my penis for an infant's.

1541 • Like

King David I feel ya, man.

1541 • Like

Copernicus Just discovered that the Earth actually revolves around the Sun.

1543 • Comment • Like

The Catholic Church hahahahah good one, but we're the center of the universe, bro.

1543 • Like

Copernicus No, we aren't.

1543 • Like

The Catholic Church wat

1543 • Like

Copernicus Would you like to see proof?

1543 • Like

The Catholic Church SHUT YOUR MOUTH.

1543 • Like

Romeo Montague So excited for tonight. Want to see my special someone. ;-)

1594 • Comment • Like

Juliet Capulet Me too, babe. I can't wait. <3 <3
1594 • Like

Romeo Montague Oh babe you're so amazing. luv u <3
1594 • Like

Juliet Capulet No you are amazing!!!1! luv u more
1594 • Like

Romeo Montague No luv u more!
1594 • Like

Mercutio Barf.
1594 • Like

Juliet Capulet was tagged in **Romeo Montague**'s album.

Yonder Window Uploads

1594 • Comment • Like

Juliet Capulet likes this.

Nurse Capulet The creepy guy watching you from the bushes is the one you want to marry?
1594 • Like

Queen Elizabeth added **Celibacy** to her Interests.
1594 • Comment • Like

John Smith Hellooo New World — at **Jamestown, Virginia** with **hundreds of colonists.**
1607 • Comment • Like

Pocahontas changed her hometown from **Just Around the Riverbend** to **Jamestown, Virginia**.
1607 • Comment • Like

Galileo My new baby.

1609 • Comment • Like

The Catholic Church wtf is that for? Whatever it is, I don't like it.
1609 • Like

Galileo It's for keeping your head in the sand.
1609 • Like

The Catholic Church Oh, really? Huh. That's cool I guess.
1609 • Like

Pocahontas likes **The Colors of the Wind**.
1614 • Comment • Like

Church of England > **Puritans** Friends, Citizens, Countrymen, thou must cease thine Puritan ways and adhere to our religion.
September 6, 1620 • Comment • Like

Puritans Forsooth, do not let these matters concern you thus, as we shall depart for fairer lands.
September 6, 1620 • Like

Church of England Doth my ears deceive me? Depart?
September 6, 1620 • Like

Puritans 'Tis true, we hath decided to take our peoples to the New World forthwith.
September 6, 1620 • Like

Church of England Thou fleest o'er the Atlantic? But why?
September 6, 1620 • Like

Puritans To be fair, because thou art a dick to us. We seek freedom of faith.
September 6, 1620 • Like

Church of England Thou ally thyself with a shitty religion.
September 6, 1620 • Like

Puritans And better ways of spelling "colour" and "favourite."
September 6, 1620 • Like

Church of England Thou art a bunch of retards.
September 6, 1620 • Like

Puritans And decent dentistry.
September 6, 1620 • Like

Church of England Thou knowest what? Thou can go fuck thyself. Go board thy Gayflower already.
September 6, 1620 • Like

Puritans Mayflower.
September 6, 1620 • Like

Church of England Whatever.
September 6, 1620 • Like

Puritans are now friends with **The Atlantic Ocean** and **Boredom.**

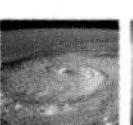 

September 6, 1620 • Comment • Like

Puritans We hath arrived! Um... somewhere.

September 6, 1620 • Comment • Like

John Smith Plymouth Bay, champ.
September 6, 1620 • Like

Puritans Ah. Forsooth.
September 6, 1620 • Like

Puritans — are at **Plymouth Bay Colony**.
September 6, 1620 • Comment • Like

Puritans I suppose this makes us the Plymouth Pilgrims.
September 6, 1620 • Like

Church of England I suppose this makes you defriended.
September 6, 1620 • Like

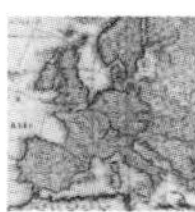

Europe Can't wait for this weekend's witch hunt!
September 6, 1620 • Comment • Like

Maiden How do you know who's a witch?
September 6, 1620 • Like

Europe Just torture a confession out of them!
September 6, 1620 • Like

Maiden That logic seems... flawed.
September 6, 1620 • Like

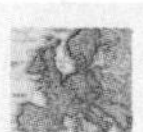

Europe That sounds like witch-talk to me.
September 6, 1620 • Like

Plymouth Pilgrims like **Buckles.**
September 6, 1620 • Comment • Like

Plymouth Pilgrims This colonizing thing is harder than it looks. Anyone know how to, like, grow food?
1621 • Comment • Like

Native Americans -sigh- ...give me a shovel, let me show you. And take off that stupid hat.
1621 • Like

Native Americans This does not bode well.

Helped by Natives, Pilgrims Survive Winter
Colonists Briefly Grateful, Soon Return to Expanding Territory

1621 • Comment • Like

Plymouth Pilgrims > Native Americans Guys, wanted to show our gratitude for helping us, you know, not die this past winter by throwing you a big potluck dinner. Whaddya say? Maybe this Thursday?
1621 • Comment • Like

Native Americans Sure! Anything we can bring?
1621 • Like

Plymouth Pilgrims Actually, yeah... maybe all the food? We're still not so good at this farming thing.
1621 • Like

Native Americans. Oh. Uh, sure. OK.
1621 • Like

Plymouth Pilgrims Fab! We'll bring gratitude. And imperialism. And foreign diseases.
1621 • Like

Native Americans What?
1621 • Like

Plymouth Pilgrims LOL totally kidding!
1621 • Like

Plymouth Pilgrims Kind of.
1621 • Like

Galileo Copernicus was right!

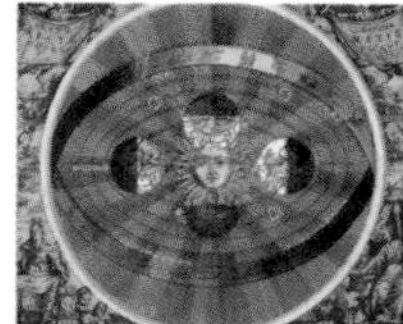
Galileo Proves Heliocentrism
Vein Bulges on Church's Forehead

 1632 • Comment • Like

Logic and **Reason** like this.

The Catholic Church You're going to regret this.
1632 • Like

Roman Inquisition > **Galileo** We need to have a little chat.
1632 • Comment • Like

Galileo At home. Will be here for a while.
1632 • Comment • Like

The Catholic Church ;-)
1632 • Like

New England is friends with **New York**, **Boston**, and **8 other cities.**

1653 • Comment • Like

England Keep it together over there, guys.

Various Obnoxious Accents Forming in New England Colonies
Broad A, Nasal Tones Catching On

 1680 • Comment • Like

---

Giacomo Casanova is now friends with **Lady Mercado** and **4 other women**. In one night.

1745 • Comment • Like

Don Juan NICE.
1745 • Like

Boston created an event.

Tea Party!
Protest unfair taxation by making the whole town smell like chamomile!

 December 16, 1773 • Comment • Like • Share • RSVP to this event

Benjamin Franklin A righteous cause! Let's hope that in the future this event isn't misappropriated by ignorant, angry white people to advocate a backwards political agenda!
December 16, 1773 • Like

The 13 Colonies are in a relationship with **King George III**, and it's complicated.

1776 • Comment • Like

King George III WHAT???? Are u serious?
1776 • Like

The 13 Colonies Don't make this harder than it already is. The relationship was long distance and too taxing.
1776 • Like

King George III So this IS about that whole "no representation" thing. Whatever. Taxes shmaxes.
1776 • Like

Thomas Jefferson If that's how you feel, then colonies shmolonies...
1776 • Like

King George III Wait, no, don't!
1776 • Like

The 13 Colonies are Single.
1776 • Comment • Like

Life, Liberty, and **The Pursuit of Happiness** like this.

King George III dammit.
1776 • Like

Thomas Jefferson Booyah.
1776 • Like

Ben Franklin lol
1776 • Like

Ben Franklin tagged **Thomas Jefferson** and **12 others** in a photo.

1776 • Comment • Like

The United States "The 13 Colonies" never rolled off the tongue.
1776 • Like

John Hancock We have GOT to do this signing thing more often. Such a blast!
1776 • Like

Thomas Jefferson We noticed.
1776 • Like

King George III created an event.

The American Revolutionary War
Because It's Pronounced "to-MAH-to"

31 1776 • Comment • Like • Share • RSVP to this event

The United States Don't forget to bring your cute wigs.
1776 • Like

France lol I got your back, America.
1776 • Like

Paul Revere Waaaaakeupppptheeeeyy'rehhhheeeerrrreee
1776 • Comment • Like

Sarah Palin likes this.

Marie Antoinette Back from a day of shopping! OMG totally excited about my new summer outfits. Big girly squeeaaaal!
1776 • Comment • Like

French Peasantry Hey, if you're shopping, mind picking up some bread? We're all out.
1776 • Like

Marie Antoinette Sorry, I'm on a diet--no carbs. Or favors for poor people. Have cake instead.
1776 • Like

Ludwig van Beethoven

Fur Elise
For a girl i know <3

1776 • Comment • Like

Elise von Rohrenbach "Just friends" means just friends, Ludwig.
1776 • Like

Ludwig van Beethoven >:-(
1776 • Like

Marie Antoinette added **Ignorance** to her Interests.
1776 • Comment • Like

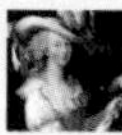

Marie Antoinette I honestly don't even know what that word means!
1776 • Like

The United States > British Army Don't let that screen door hit you on the way out.
1783 • Comment • Like

Wolfgang Amadeus Mozart > Beethoven Great symphony man, really liked it. I wrote one just like it once. When I was six.
1783 • Comment • Like

Ludwig van Beethoven >:-(
1783 • Like

French Peasantry

Revolution in France!
Poor Revolt Against Exploitation by Rich, Can't Really Blame Them

August 18, 1792 • Comment • Like

Democracy likes this.

Marie Antoinette Is this like a masquerade ball or something?
August 18, 1792 • Like

French Peasantry Not quite. It's a party where we'll introduce you to the Guillotine.
August 18, 1792 • Like

Marie Antoinette Ooo, Guillotine? Is he like a new designer?
August 18, 1792 • Like

Marie Antoinette is listed as separated from **Her Head**.
August 18, 1792 • Comment • Like

The French Army has discovered the Rosetta Stone.

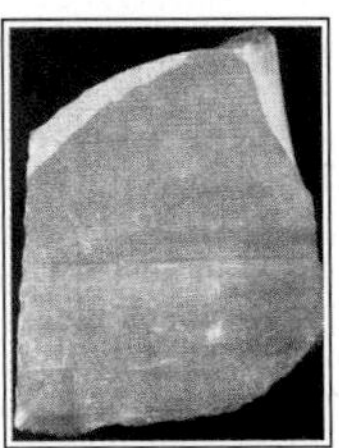

1799 • Comment • Like

Dr. Watson This is astonishing. Have you translated it yet?
1799 • Like

Professor Picard I have. It's this strange, rambling tale about an unlikable teenage girl who starts at a new high school, completely falls for this creepy kid in her class with pale sparkly skin who fixates on her and her "smell," but it turns out he's a vampire. She's not afraid of him, so they fall in love but, for shockingly unrealistic reasons, never have sex.
1799 • Like

Dr. Watson Lame.
1799 • Like

Professor Picard Yep.
1799 • Like

The United States > Meriwether Lewis This weekend, dude. ROAD TRIP. U down!?
1804 • Comment • Like

Meriwether Lewis Woo! Sure, where to?
1804 • Like

The United States Dunno!
1804 • Like

Meriwether Lewis Atlantic City maybe?
1804 • Like

The United States No no, like literally "I don't know" because it's never been explored.
1804 • Like

Meriwether Lewis Wha?
1804 • Like

The United States Well it's not so much a road trip as it is a two-year expedition into the unknown. In fact I'm preeeeeetty certain you won't encounter a single road the entire time.
1804 • Like

Meriwether Lewis Uh...
1804 • Like

The United States You leave Tuesday. Buy some oxen and a boat or whatever, and bring that Clark friend of yours.
1804 • Like

William Clark Fuuuuuuuuuu
1804 • Like

Napoleon Bonaparte Victory. An extra ration of wine for my fine soldiers.
1804 • Comment • Like

Soldier Nice! Always looking out for the little guy.
1804 • Like

Napoleon Bonaparte "Little"?
1804 • Like

Napoleon Bonaparte What do you mean, "little"? Like midget little? Like I amuse you?
1804 • Like

Soldier No no! I just... oh god.
1804 • Like

Napoleon Bonaparte I'm kidding, dude. Go get drunk and name-drop at the parties.
1804 • Like

Napoleon Bonaparte Invading Asia.
1804 • Comment • Like

General Sir, I think you're falling victim to one of the classic blunders.
1804 • Like

Napoleon Bonaparte What? Going against a Sicilian when death is on the line?
1804 • Like

General No, the other one.
1804 • Like

Napoleon Bonaparte Pff. Russia is lovely in winter.
1804 • Like

Nietzsche > God Whoa, I thought you were dead.
1810 • Comment • Like

Joan Osborne And I was wondering if you're one of us.
1810 • Like

God Like, a stranger on a bus or something?
1810 • Like

Joan Osborne Yeah, actually.
1810 • Like

Ludwig van Beethoven WOULD EVERYONE KINDLY SPEAK UP

1820 • Comment • Like

Andrew Jackson signed the **Indian Removal Act**.

1830 • Comment • Like

Native American not cool

1830 • Like

Andrew Jackson Unless ur white

1830 • Like

The U.S. Treasury tagged **Andrew Jackson** in a photo.

1830 • Comment • Like

Andrew Jackson likes this.

Native American — is on **The Trail of Tears**.

1830 • Comment • Like

Andrew Jackson kthxbai

1830 • Like

Andrew Jackson and **Aaron Burr** added **Duels** to their Interests.

1830 • Comment • Like

Aaron Burr This is what happens when you insult my honor.

1830 • Like

Alexander Hamilton What honor?

1830 • Like

Thomas Jefferson lol
1830 • Like

The Alamo Can't say I'm confident about these odds.
1836 • Comment • Like

General Santa Anna Looks good from where I'm standing.
1836 • Like

Davy Crockett GET SOME

1836 • Comment • Like

Texas likes this.

Texas Remember the Alamo!
1836 • Comment • Like

Jingoism likes this.

Denzel Washington And the Titans!
1836 • Like

Earth Wind and Fire And the 21st niiiiiiight of Septembah!
1836 • Like

Charles Darwin added **Theory of Evolution** to his Interests.
1838 • Comment • Like

Alfred Russel Wallace and **Thomas Huxley** like this.

The Pope Evowhat?
1838 • Like

Charles Darwin This could get awkward.
1838 • Like

Charles Darwin Call me crazy, but it appears that all living organisms have evolved from more basic forms over the millenia.
1838 • Comment • Like

The Catholic Church Hahaha, yeah bro ur crazy.
1838 • Like

Charles Darwin No, seriously. This is backed by observable evidence.
1838 • Like

The Catholic Church Lol alright crazy man, that's enough.
1838 • Like

Charles Darwin In fact, I think it's very likely humans have evolved from primates.
1838 • Like

The Catholic Church SHUT YOUR FACE. SHUT IT RIGHT NOW.
1838 • Like

Samuel Morse Invented new communication technology -STOP- Very excited, calling it the "Telegraph" -STOP- Give my love to Mother -STOP-
May 24, 1844 • Comment • Like

Elizabeth Donner Well great. The pass is closed for the winter, so we're just gonna have to wait this one out. Should be fine, just wish we had brought a little more food.
1846 • Comment • Like

Elizabeth Donner OK maybe a lot more food.
1846 • Like

James Donner > Elizabeth Donner I am so OVER this. All the snow, the starvation, the dying, the whole expedition. I'm sick of it. Stick a fork in me, I'm done.
1847 • Comment • Like

Elizabeth Donner ...
1847 • Like

James Donner Not like that.
1847 • Like

James Marshall Working up at the lumber mill. Another day, another dollar. Literally.
1849 • Comment • Like

James Marshall What in the dandy hornswaggle? I do believe I've struck gold!
1849 • Like

Sneaky Pete Balderdash! Daguerreotype or it didn't happen!
1849 • Like

James Marshall

1849 • Comment • Like

Sneaky Pete By Jove you're right!
1849 • Like

James Marshall We could make a hundred dollars!
1849 • Like

Sneaky Pete A hundred dollars? A hundred dollars isn't cool. You know what's cool? A *thousand* dollars.
1849 • Like

James Marshall HOLY SHIT, GOLD GET YOUR ASSES TO CALIFORNIA, PEOPLE
1849 • Comment • Like

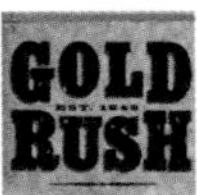

80,000 people changed their current city to **San Francisco, California**.
1849 • Comment • Like

Charles Darwin Published!

The Origin of Species,
By Means of Natural Selection
Backed Up by Oodles of Scientific Evidence and Fossil Records

 1850 • Comment • Like

The World Whooaaaa.
1850 • Like

The Catholic Church SON OF A BITCH
1850 • Like

The United States

Citing Allergy to Excitement, America Adopts Baseball as National Pastime

 1856 • Comment • Like

Peanuts and Crackerjacks like this.

The Home Team We didn't win.
1856 • Like

The United States Shame.
1856 • Like

Abraham Lincoln signed the **Emancipation Proclamation.**
January 1, 1863 • Comment • Like

Plantation Owner wtf!? u can't just take away a man's rights like that! U treatin' us like animals!
January 1, 1863 • Like

Slave Please take a step back and read what you just wrote.
January 1, 1863 • Like

Plantation Owner hey, did I say u could talk?
January 1, 1863 • Like

Slave The hypocrisy here is just astounding.
January 1, 1863 • Like

Plantation Owner Hypowhat? Is that slave talk or somethin'?
January 1, 1863 • Like

Cornelius Vanderbilt NBD.

Vanderbilt Buys Saturn
Railroad Tycoon Declares Planet's Rings Will "Look Swell" on Mantel

January 1, 1863 • Comment • Like

Abraham Lincoln — is in **Gettysburg, Pennsylvania** with the **Union Army**.
November 19, 1863 • Comment • Like

Abraham Lincoln You bring the speech?
November 19, 1863 • Like

Speechwriter Uh, I thought you had it.
November 19, 1863 • Like

Abraham Lincoln You gotta be kidding me.
November 19, 1863 • Like

Speechwriter I'm sorry, sir. I don't have it.
November 19, 1863 • Like

Abraham Lincoln I can't... We'll do it live.
November 19, 1863 • Like

Speechwriter OK.... um...
November 19, 1863 • Like

Abraham Lincoln WE'LL DO IT LIVE. FUCK IT. I'LL WRITE IT, AND WE'LL DO IT LIVE.
November 19, 1863 • Like

Abraham Lincoln likes **Stove Pipe Hats** and **Not Smiling**.
April 9, 1865 • Comment • Like

Robert E. Lee — is at **Appomattox** with **Ulysses S. Grant**.
April 9, 1865 • Comment • Like

Ulysses S. Grant Sooo we're cool, right?
April 9, 1865 • Like

Robert E. Lee Yeeah... we're cool.
April 9, 1865 • Like

Ulysses S. Grant You boys promise not to hold a grudge?
April 9, 1865 • Like

Robert E. Lee Promise.
April 9, 1865 • Like

Ulysses S. Grant Promise your descendants won't fly Confederate flags from their pickup trucks as a sign of "Southern pride" even though it's the banner of slavery?
April 9, 1865 • Like

Robert E. Lee One step at a time.
April 9, 1865 • Like

The Union is now friends with **Georgia**, **Virginia**, and **9 other states**.

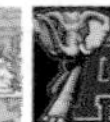

April 9, 1865 • Comment • Like

The United States likes this.

Abraham Lincoln Going to the theater tonight with the missus... got private box seats, baby!
April 14, 1865 • Comment • Like

John Wilkes Booth likes this.

Industrial Revolution

Advancements in machinery allowed manufacturing, transportation, and agriculture to boom, triggering a level of socioeconomic growth that the world had never seen. Factories sprung up, the steam engine gained steam, and people ceased their agrarian toil and flocked to cities to begin their first "9 to 5"—though admittedly it was less "9 to 5" and more "9 to Sleep at Your Loom, Woman."

A 140-hour workweek wasn't without its perks, however: free bandages for bleeding fingers, sick leave for the dead, a 15-minute break for pregnant women to perform a standing birth, and prior to their first shift newborns were allowed to dry. It was the best of times, it was the worst of times. Mostly the worst of times.

Through hardship nations prospered. England grew rich off its export of textiles, iron, sooty-faced orphans, and depressing literature. America pushed westward with its railways and became the world's premier tobacco supplier, kicking off a pretty illustrious career helping folks die.

The Industrial Revolution was the first step in modernization, and the world has never looked back. Except on *Antiques Roadshow,* only on PBS.

Union Pacific Railroad — is at **Promontory, Utah** with **Central Pacific Railroad**.

1868 • Comment • Like

Leland Stanford With that done, I'm off to found a university.

Transcontinental Railroad Complete! Industrialist Leland Stanford Joins Railways with Blingin' Gold Spike

1868 • Comment • Like

Union Pacific Railroad Here's to the next century of rail travel!

1868 • Like

Henry Ford heh heh

1868 • Like

Alexander Graham Bell Can you hear me now?

1874 • Comment • Like

General Custer — is at **Little Big Horn** with the **7th Cavalry Regiment**.

June 25, 1876 • Comment • Like

General Custer Chased off some savages, all is quiet at Little Big Horn.

June 25, 1876 • Like

General Custer Boy, it's really quiet.

June 25, 1876 • Like

General Custer Like, too quiet.

June 25, 1876 • Like

New York Times

Motion Picturegraph Show Wows Audiences "Amazing" Two-Second Loop of Horse Running; "Man Doing Somersaults" Sequel Planned

June 19, 1878 • Comment • Like

Eadweard Muybridge likes this.

Hollywood, California I have a great idea.
June 19, 1878 • Like

Thomas Edison Just had a *bright* idea!

October 22, 1879 • Comment • Like

Nikola Tesla If only your puns were as good as your inventions.
October 22, 1879 • Like

Thomas Edison You're just jealous because you don't *shine* like me.
October 22, 1879 • Like

Nikola Tesla Stop.
October 22, 1879 • Like

John Pemberton Threw some ingredients together to make a little tonic. Some carbonated water, a bunch of sugar, some cola nut. Anyone want to try?
October 22, 1879 • Comment • Like

Lab Technician It's tasty, but it's missing... something...
October 22, 1879 • Like

John Pemberton Just added a bunch of coca leaf extract. Try that.
October 22, 1879 • Like

Lab Technician OkWOWmuchbetterIfeelgreat.
October 22, 1879 • Like

Marty McFly Where the hell am I now WHOA INDIANS

September 5, 1885 • Comment • Like

Indians WHOA METAL DEMON
September 5, 1885 • Like

Helen Keller slkef n2 0Dd cn vsdlk3 lkjdf.
June 15, 1890 • Comment • Like

Annie Sullivan This is going be tough.
June 15, 1890 • Like

The United States

President William McKinley
Assassinated
Nation Mourns Death

September 6, 1901 • Comment • Like

The United States He will never be forgotten.
September 6, 1901 • Like

The United States For a little while, at least.
September 6, 1901 • Like

The United States I mean, let's be honest, 110 years from now, say "William McKinley" to most Americans and you'll be met with blank stares.
September 6, 1901 • Like

The United States I don't mean to be insensitive, of course. But I just see some future wiseass writer trying to make a joke about the whole assassination, and yet nobody knows who this McKinley guy was! The writer would have to make a big, wordy production to explain the joke, it'd undoubtedly fail, and he'd just have to apologize for even writing such lousy stuff.
September 6, 1901 • Like

The United States btw I'm sorry.
September 6, 1901 • Like

Picasso added **The Color Blue** and **Nudes** to his Interests.
February 2, 1902 • Comment • Like

Railroad > Ocean Liners party's over, bro.

Wright Brothers Create Aeroplane Machine
Nation, Birds "Astonished to See Man Fly"

 December 17, 1903 • Comment • Like

Zeppelin Impractical.
December 17, 1903 • Like

Humpty Dumpty Great view from where I'm sitting.
April 11, 1904 • Comment • Like

Humpty Dumpty OH SHI
April 11, 1904 • Like

Humpty Dumpty > King's Horses Fellas, a little help?
April 11, 1904 • Comment • Like

King's Horses Sorry, man, we did our best.
April 11, 1904 • Like

King's Men Ditto.
April 11, 1904 • Like

Humpty Dumpty -sigh-
April 11, 1904 • Like

King's Men's Soooooo... omelets then?
April 11, 1904 • Like

San Francisco Giant earthquake just rolled through, and now fires are raging all over the place.

April 18, 1906 • Comment • Like

Oscar Wilde You'll be flaming long after the fires go out, honey.
April 18, 1906 • Like

San Andreas Fault Sorry. That's my fault... er, my fault's fault. You get what I'm saying.
April 18, 1906 • Like

Picasso added **Cubes** to his Interests.
April 18, 1906 • Comment • Like

Henry Ford

Ford Motor Company Unveils "Automobile" Machine
Carriage Makers Go Home, Kick Dog, Quietly Weep

September 27, 1908 • Comment • Like

Ford Model T > Horse Sorry, man. I feel bad about this.
September 27, 1908 • Comment • Like

Horse Why? I don't have to work anymore.
September 27, 1908 • Like

Ford Model T Oh. Huh. How are you gonna spend your time now?
September 27, 1908 • Like

Horse I dunno. I'll chill in pastures. Be an object of affection for young girls. Be an object of desire for women who like to braid hair. Graze. Maybe show up in a parade, do some pooping. Whatevs.
September 27, 1908 • Like

Chicago Cubs And it won't be long before we win another. hollaaaa

Chicago Cubs Win!
1908 World Series Champions

October 14, 1908 • Comment • Like

Theodore Roosevelt Presidency done. Off to shoot an elephant, and/or anything else that moves. Laterzzz.
March 25, 1909 • Comment • Like

R.M.S. Titanic Here's to a flawless maiden voyage.
April 14, 1912 • Comment • Like

Hubris and Fate like this.

R.M.S. Titanic > Security Little help--crazy dude at the bow yelling about how he's the king of the world.
April 14, 1912 • Comment • Like

Security We're on it.
April 14, 1912 • Like

R.M.S. Titanic > Iceberg Out of the way, fella.
April 14, 1912 • Comment • Like

Iceberg I can't move for you, sir.
April 14, 1912 • Like

Titanic It's like that?
April 14, 1912 • Like

Iceberg No, I literally cannot move on my own accord. I'm an iceberg.
April 14, 1912 • Like

R.M.S. Titanic Bonked an iceberg, no big deal tho when you're UNSINKABLE.
April 14, 1912 • Comment • Like

Iceberg You sure?
April 14, 1912 • Like

Titanic Yeah. Why?
April 14, 1912 • Like

Iceberg Give it a second.
April 14, 1912 • Like

Titanic ...??
April 14, 1912 • Like

Titanic You son of a bitch.
April 14, 1912 • Like

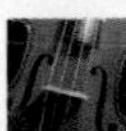

Titanic String Quartet You want us to stop playing?
April 14, 1912 • Like

Titanic Nope. You're coming with me.
April 14, 1912 • Like

New York Times

Titanic Sinks!
Lost to the Depths: 1,517 Souls, Blossoming Love Between Rich Girl and Poor Boy

April 14, 1912 • Comment • Like

Titanic checked in to the **Ocean Floor**.
April 14, 1912 • Comment • Like

James Cameron likes this.

Germany, **Britain**, and **4 other European Powers** like **Nationalism** and **Imperialism**.
1913 • Comment • Like

The United States Eaaaasy, fellas.
1913 • Like

Archduke Franz Ferdinand up late working on uniting the empire, and trying to figure out if my mustache can get any more awesome. Boioioioing!
June 28, 1914 • Comment • Like

Archduke Franz Ferdinand checked in to **Sarajevo**.
June 28, 1914 • Comment • Like

Gavrilo Princip > **Archduke Franz Ferdinand** Taste lead, TYRANT!
June 28, 1914 • Comment • Like

Serbia > **Gavrilo Princip** why why WHY did you do that!?!!?!!?!!
June 28, 1914 • Comment • Like

Gavrilo Princip Oh c'mon, he was an oppressor. What's the worst that can happen?
June 28, 1914 • Like

Austria-Hungary

Austria-Hungary Declares War on Serbia
World Winces:
"This Might Snowball"

June 28, 1914 • Comment • Like

Gavrilo Princip Oh.
June 28, 1914 • Like

Serbia Yeah.
June 28, 1914 • Like

Germany is in a domestic partnership with **Austria-Hungary.**
June 28, 1914 • Comment • Like

Germany > Russia We're at war!
August 1914 • Comment • Like

Germany > France We're at war!
August 1914 • Comment • Like

Belgium > Germany We're at war!
August 1914 • Comment • Like

Britain > Germany We're at war!
August 1914 • Comment • Like

France > Britain We're at... wait, no, sorry.
August 1914 • Comment • Like

France > Austria-Hungary We're at war!
August 1914 • Comment • Like

Britain > Austria-Hungary We're at war!
August 1914 • Comment • Like

Germany > Russia We're at war!
August 1914 • Comment • Like

Russia Already sent that to me.
August 1914 • Like

Germany oh right.
August 1914 • Like

Germany > United States We're at war!
August 1914 • Comment • Like

United States Is someone writing all this down?
August 1914 • Like

Germany That's a good idea actually.
August 1914 • Like

The London Star Tribune Herald Sentinel Ledger Times

Everyone Declares War on Everyone Else
No, Really: Literally Everyone Is All Up in This Shit

August 1914 • Comment • Like

France, **Britain**, and **Germany** like **Trenches**.
August 1914 • Comment • Like

French Soldiers added **Dying** to their Interests.
August 1914 • Comment • Like

German Soldiers like this.

Britain Jolly good day! Gained 18 feet on the front, only 34,000 dead.
September 12, 1918 • Comment • Like

Attrition likes this.

France Hey, not bad! Gained 14 inches, lost 8,000. Oh wait.... carry the 1... no, that should be 80,000. Not great, but not bad either.
September 12, 1918 • Like

French Soldiers -sigh-
September 12, 1918 • Like

Britain Check out my new wheels. Er, treads.

Tank!

September 12, 1918 • Comment • Like

France coooOOOOoool
September 12, 1918 • Like

Germany — checked in to **Ypres, France.**
September 12, 1918 • Comment • Like

Germany added **Poison Gas** to its Interests.
September 12, 1918 • Comment • Like

Germany Suck it!

Poison Gas

September 12, 1918 • Comment • Like

British Soldiers What's that smell?
September 12, 1918 • Like

French Soldiers Don't breaaAGGHH
September 12, 1918 • Like

New York Times

Analysts Predict: Bear Market for Empires, Monarchies Democracies, Socialist Republics

September 12, 1918 • Comment • Like

Ottoman Empire Hm.
September 12, 1918 • Like

German Empire Meddling scum! This isn't good.
September 12, 1918 • Like

British Empire Not if ur on the right team! #goAllies
September 12, 1918 • Like

T. E. Lawrence changed his name to **Lawrence of Arabia.**
September 12, 1918 • Comment • Like

Arabia likes this.

German Empire OK, I'm running out of space to bury people.
November 11, 1918 • Comment • Like

France Me too.
November 11, 1918 • Like

Russia I got plenty of space, I just don't have anyone left to do the burying.
November 11, 1918 • Like

German Empire > The Allies Sooo, can we get a time-out? Like, a permanent one?
November 11, 1918 • Comment • Like

The Allies Gladly. But we're gonna need you to fork over some cash, and we're redrawing Europe's borders. In case it wasn't obvious, you're gonna lose a lot of land.
November 11, 1918 • Like

Austro-Hungarian Empire lol
November 11, 1918 • Like

The Allies don't laugh: you're not going to exist.
November 11, 1918 • Like

Austro-Hungarian Empire ouch
November 11, 1918 • Like

The Allies created an event.

Treaty of Versailles
Who wants a piping hot piece of land from the losers?

31 June 28, 1919 • Comment • Like • Share • RSVP to this event

Poland and **Cartographers** like this.

Europe changed its profile picture.
June 28, 1919 • Comment • Like

Poland > Germany Thanks for the land, bro.
June 28, 1919 • Comment • Like

Czechoslovakia likes this.

Germany This is humiliating.
June 28, 1919 • Like

Adolf Hitler We should talk.
June 28, 1919 • Like

Women's Suffrage

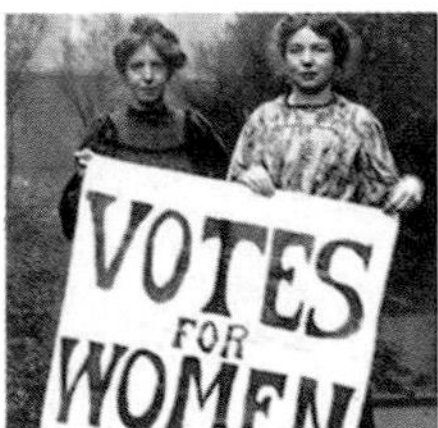

Women Granted Right to Vote
Men Confused How They'll Do That from Kitchen

1919 • Comment • Like

Susan B. Anthony Still got a ways to go, ladies.
1919 • Like

Sexism You mean from the kitchen to the laundry room?
1919 • Like

The 18th Amendment created an event.

Prohibition!
Awesome good times with arms-length dancing, polite conversation, healthy juice refreshments!

31 January 17, 1920 • Comment • Like • Share • RSVP to this event

The United States wow, sounds like a blast.
January 17, 1920 • Like

Prohibition Totally! You coming?
January 17, 1920 • Like

The United States oh I wouldn't miss it for the ZZZZZZZZ. Yeah right, I'll be down at the speakeasy, drinking until I walk into a wall. Good night, enjoy your juice. Weirdo.
January 17, 1920 • Like

Al Capone First round's on me.
January 17, 1920 • Like

Jay Gatsby created the event **Another Obscenely Sumptuous and Utterly Shallow Party, Darlings.**

31 September 9, 1922 • Comment • Like • Share • RSVP to this event

Jay Gatsby Maybe someone will actually know who I am this time!! Like Daisy Buchanan!
September 9, 1922 • Like

Daisy Buchanan > Tom Buchanan Let me drive, please?
September 9, 1922 • Comment • Like

Tom Buchanan Fine, you little hussy, drive if you like.
September 9, 1922 • Like

Nick Carraway You guys are like the *original* douchebags.
September 9, 1922 • Like

King Tut Hey..... where the hell is all my stuff?
November 4, 1922 • Comment • Like

Carmen Sandiego likes this.

Georgia O'Keeffe Just finished a new painting of a ladyflower.

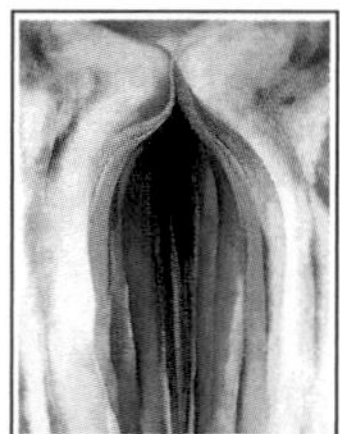

June 6, 1926 • Comment • Like

Georgia O'Keeffe Er, flower. I mean flower.
June 6, 1926 • Like

Frida Kahlo We should hang out.
June 6, 1926 • Like

Los Angeles Times

Universal Pictures Sends
Giant Letters in Low Orbit
Execs: "Sure Beats a Lion Roaring"

October 9, 1926 • Comment • Like

Leprechaun — checked in to **End of the Rainbow Bar and Grill.**

October 9, 1926 • Comment • Like

Leprechaun At the local dive. If anyone wants to join, this place makes great margaritas. They're like a sweet little pot of gold. I'll buy you one. Happy hour is only on for another 20, so chop chop.

October 9, 1926 • Like

Irishman Well that explains *that* rumor.

October 9, 1926 • Like

Charles Lindbergh — checked in to **Roosevelt Field, New York.**

May 20, 1927 • Comment • Like

Spirit of St. Louis Let's do this.

May 20, 1927 • Like

Charles Lindbergh — checked in to **Le Bourget Field, Paris.**

May 21, 1927 • Comment • Like

150,000 people like this.

The Atlantic Ocean Damn, Chaz. Not bad.

May 21, 1927 • Like

The Pacific Ocean Double or nothing?

May 21, 1927 • Like

New York Stock Exchange Chilling at Dow Jones's place. Getting high off speculation and a credit bubble, woooo!

October 28, 1929 • Comment • Like

Dow Jones Wow dude, I am so high. Wait, should we order pizza? OMG pizza sounds amazing. So do blue chip stocks though. Ahh I can't decide!

October 28, 1929 • Like

New York Stock Exchange Lol dude get both! And Twizzlers.

October 28, 1929 • Like

Banks Uh, you sure you want to post this publicly?
October 28, 1929 • Like

Investors Wait, what credit bubble?!
October 28, 1929 • Like

Dow Jones > New York Stock Exchange Bro what the hell happened last night? I think I lost my keys and, like, 30% of my value.
October 28, 1929 • Comment • Like

Banks Really? Wow that's really surprising considering you were HIGH ON A CREDIT BUBBLE, but no, it's cool, I'll just kick back and ride the panic into sweet oblivion.
October 28, 1929 • Like

Dow Jones and **New York Stock Exchange** created the event **Black Tuesday**.
31 October 29, 1929 • Comment • Like • Share • RSVP to this event

Investors Oh no.
October 29, 1929 • Like

Banks Soooo um, anyone have a spare $30 billion or so?
October 29, 1929 • Like

Investors Nonononono
October 29, 1929 • Like

The Roaring '20s changed its name to **The Great Depression**.
October 29, 1929 • Comment • Like

Investors NOOOOOOOOOOOO
October 29, 1929 • Like

Sears and Roebuck

New Fashions for Spring:
Rags, Empty Barrels
Poor Is the New Black!

October 29, 1929 • Comment • Like

Charlie Chaplin

Small Mustaches: All the Rage

February 8, 1930 • Comment • Like

Lita Grey You look good, Charlie.
February 8, 1930 • Like

Charlie Chaplin ;-D
February 8, 1930 • Like

Adolf Hitler Nice article.
February 8, 1930 • Like

Charlie Chaplin 8-\
February 8, 1930 • Like

Al Jolson > Charlie Chaplin Thought you should see this.

New "Talkie" Movies Usher in New Era
Future of Silent Films Uncertain

February 8, 1930 • Comment • Like

Charlie Chaplin :-O
February 8, 1930 • Like

Buster Keaton :-(
February 8, 1930 • Like

Al Jolson You guys keep that up even online, eh?
February 8, 1930 • Like

Alcatraz Prison Open for business.
January 1, 1931 • Comment • Like

Azkaban Prison You're such an inspiration!
January 1, 1931 • Like

New York Times

Tallest in the World!
Empire State Building Opens, Attracting Crowds, Huge Gorilla

May 1, 1931 • Comment • Like

Ann Darrow FML
May 1, 1931 • Like

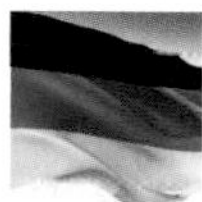

Germany Just tried on nationalism and I gotta say... it feels preeeetty good.
May 1, 1931 • Comment • Like

Adolf Hitler likes this.

Charles Lindbergh

Kidnapped: Infant Son of
American Hero Charles Lindbergh
Furious Nation Looking
for Scapego... Er, Suspect

March 1, 1932 • Comment • Like

Babe Ruth Next pitch? Home run. Thataway.
October 1, 1932 • Comment • Like

New York Yankees Aaaaand boom goes the dynamite.
October 1, 1932 • Like

New York Times

Nation Asks Brother for Spare Dime
Declares It Once Built Railroad, "Made It Race Against Time"

November 8, 1932 • Comment • Like

Al Jolson likes this.

Neville Chamberlain Let's just not step on his toes.

New "Hitler" Guy Assumes Power in Germany
World a Little Creeped Out: Not Nearly as Adorable as Charlie Chaplin

January 30, 1933 • Comment • Like

President Franklin D. Roosevelt We have nothing to fear... but fear itself! And maybe some starvation. Also, foreclosures and scabies. Beyond that though, it's just fear.
March 4, 1933 • Comment • Like

The New York Times

President to Hold "Fireside Chat"
Nation Fears "Really Awkward Bird and Bees" Talk

March 12, 1933 • Comment • Like

President Roosevelt Go get wasted, folks. Lord knows these days we could all use a beer.

Prohibition Ends!
Celebrants Take to Streets, Singing Incorrect Lyrics, Dancing Like Idiots

March 22, 1933 • Comment • Like

Everyone likes this, except **assholes.**

Organized Crime Curses!
March 22, 1933 • Like

Howard Hughes is friends with **Katharine Hepburn, Ava Gardner**, and **4 other starlets.**

March 22, 1933 • Comment • Like

Howard Hughes likes this. A lot.

Loch Ness Monster "Why not go to the surface" they say. "What's the worst that can happen?" they say.

May 2, 1933 • Comment • Like

Bigfoot I feel ya.
May 2, 1933 • Like

Poland Yay, here's to peace!

Germany Agrees to Non-Aggression Pact with Poland
Hitler Signs with Ceremonial Crossed-Fingers Technique

January 22, 1934 • Comment • Like

Poland likes this.

Germany Peace indeed. ;-|
January 22, 1934 • Like

Poland ha, what's the wink for?
January 22, 1934 • Like

Germany Hm? Ooh look, a pretty bird.
January 22, 1934 • Like

Clyde Barrow > Bonnie Parker Wanna go for a drive, babe?
May 23, 1934 • Comment • Like

Texas Law Enforcement likes this.

Germany changed its profile picture.
August 2, 1934 • Comment • Like

Jews aaaaand *that* is why we need the dislike button.
August 2, 1934 • Like

President Franklin D. Roosevelt So.... who wants to build a fuckload of dams?

Works Progress Administration

April 8, 1935 • Comment • Like

T. E. Lawrence Beautiful day for a ride...
May 19, 1935 • Comment • Like

Oklahoma

Midwest "Dust Bowl" Crisis Produces Record Harvest of Iconic Photographs, Novels, Folk Songs

June 7, 1935 • Comment • Like

Woody Guthrie and **John Steinbeck** like this.

Abraham Lincoln, George Washington, and **Thomas Jefferson** were tagged in **Theodore Roosevelt's** album.

Face on Currency < Face on Mountain

July 4, 1936 • Comment • Like

Team America likes this.

Indiana Jones

August 8, 1936 • Comment • Like

Indiana Jones Like stealing candy from a ... wait. Uh oh.
August 8, 1936 • Like

Hindenburg — checked in to **Lakehurst, New Jersey.**

May 6, 1937 • Comment • Like

Hindenburg Just gonna moor to the BURNING FIRE HOLY GOD NO
May 6, 1937 • Comment • Like

The Humanity! dislikes this.

Herbert Morrison All me, baby

Hindenburg Crash Produces Legendary Radio Broadcast
"Some of the Most Thrilling Radio I've Ever Heard" Says Listener

Also, 37 People Killed

 May 6, 1937 • Comment • Like

---

Lennie Small added **Soft Things** to his Interests.
June 18, 1937 • Comment • Like

Mouse AGH
June 18, 1937 • Like

Puppy ARHGK
June 18, 1937 • Like

Curley's Wife AKGH
June 18, 1937 • Like

George Milton Hey bud, why don't you look over yonder and hold still while I tell you about the rabbits.
June 18, 1937 • Like

Amelia Earhart — checked in to **Somewhere Over the Pacific.**
July 2, 1937 • Comment • Like

Amelia Earhart Soooo I think I might be lost.
July 2, 1937 • Comment • Like

Sexism Shocker.
July 2, 1937 • Like

Amelia Earhart created an event.

Help a Sister Out!
Your friend Amelia wants to land! Come help her do it, and she'll owe you one, and probably her life! yaaaay

31 July 2, 1937 • Comment • Like • Share • RSVP to this event

---

Amelia Earhart created an event.

Seriously, Anyone... Help.
Your friend Amelia would like you to join her in making sure she doesn't become a historical mystery!

31 July 2, 1937 • Comment • Like • Share • RSVP to this event

The Pacific Ocean I'll be there.
July 2, 1937 • Like

Amelia Earhart Not helpful.
July 2, 1937 • Like

Orson Welles

Breaking: Strange Meteorite Lands in New Jersey
Likely Origin: Mars

October 30, 1938 • Comment • Like

H. G. Wells likes this.

Orson Welles Posting updates as they come in.
October 30, 1938 • Like

Public Whoa....
October 30, 1938 • Like

Orson Welles News bulletins are saying it seems to be not a meteorite but something... extraterrestrial. And it's humming.
October 30, 1938 • Like

Orson Welles And now... now it's opening.
October 30, 1938 • Like

Public !!
October 30, 1938 • Like

Orson Welles My god, an alien ship! It's incinerating everything and everyone in it's sight! My god, run! Save yourselves! It's a war of the worlds!
October 30, 1938 • Like

Public AHHHHH
October 30, 1938 • Like

Orson Welles lol JK
October 30, 1938 • Like

Public WHAT IS WRONG WITH YOU!
October 30, 1938 • Like

Orson Welles lol
October 30, 1938 • Like

H. G. Wells lol
October 30, 1938 • Like

Steven Spielberg lol
October 30, 1938 • Like

Albert Hofmann Little late-night lab work. Art is pouring us gin and tonics in some beakers, and then it's down to business.
November 16, 1938 • Comment • Like

Albert Hofmann > Arthur Stoll Accidentally dropped some of that lysergic acid in my cocktail.
November 16, 1938 • Comment • Like

Arthur Stoll The LSD? I don't think it's harmful.
November 16, 1938 • Like

Albert Hofmann Phew. Tastes a little bitter, but yeah, otherwise no side effeWHOA
November 16, 1938 • Like

Arthur Stoll Everything OK?
November 16, 1938 • Like

Albert Hofmann Fantastic. Feel great. The walls though, they seem to be melting into... rainbows? You seeing this?
November 16, 1938 • Like

Arthur Stoll What?! No!
November 16, 1938 • Like

Albert Hofmann Shame. Now there's a double rainbow.
November 16, 1938 • Like

Arthur Stoll Across the sky?
November 16, 1938 • Like

Albert Hofmann All the way.
November 16, 1938 • Like

Grail Knight > Indiana Jones Wise choice, bro.
February 19, 1939 • Comment • Like

Henry Jones likes this, but please hurry back.

Hitler is friends with **Benito Mussolini** and **Joseph Stalin**.

February 19, 1939 • Comment • Like

Mahatma Gahndi > Adolf Hitler You're not gonna do anything crazy, right?
July 23, 1939 • Comment • Like

Adolf Hitler A census taker once tried to test me... remind me to tell you about it sometime.
July 23, 1939 • Like

Poland > Germany Yo homie! What's with all the tanks?
July 23, 1939 • Comment • Like

Adolf Hitler Don't worry about it.
July 23, 1939 • Like

New York Times

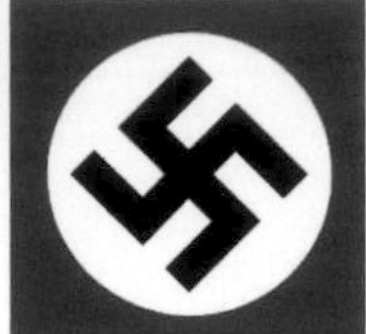

Germany, Soviet Union Agree to Non-Aggression Pact
Poland "Has Bad Feeling About This"

August 10, 1939 • Comment • Like

Soviet Union So, we're cool, right?
August 10, 1939 • Like

Adolf Hitler Sure. We're cool. ;-|
August 10, 1939 • Like

Soviet Union Why the wink?
August 10, 1939 • Like

German Army — checked in to **Poland** with the **Soviet Army**.
September 1, 1939 • Comment • Like

Poland WHAT
September 1, 1939 • Like

Hitler SIKE
September 1, 1939 • Like

Soviet Union LOL
September 1, 1939 • Like

Britain WTF
September 1, 1939 • Like

Neville Chamberlain > Adolf Hitler Listen, old boy, we've had enough of your churlish poppycock. It appears we're headed for fisticuffs.
September 1, 1939 • Comment • Like

Poland likes this.

Adolf Hitler I have no idea what he just said.
September 1, 1939 • Like

Soviet Union Wanna say that was a declaration of war. Not sure.
September 1, 1939 • Like

Albert Einstein > President Franklin D. Roosevelt Need to talk to you. I think we could end this war by splitting the atom.
October 11, 1939 • Comment • Like

President Franklin D. Roosevelt The atom? You mean the smallest thing known to man?
October 11, 1939 • Like

Albert Einstein Yes.
October 11, 1939 • Like

President Franklin D. Roosevelt ...you're high, aren't you?
October 11, 1939 • Like

Albert Einstein Just hear me out.
October 11, 1939 • Like

Adolf Hitler Blitz...
April 1940 • Comment • Like

German Army — checked in to **Belgium**.
April 1940 • Comment • Like

German Army — checked in to **Luxembourg**.
April 1940 • Comment • Like

German Army — checked in to **Norway**.
April 1940 • Comment • Like

German Army checked in to **France**.

April 1940 • Comment • Like

Adolf Hitler ...krieg!

April 1940 • Comment • Like

Neville Chamberlain Oh dear.

April 1940 • Like

France Do-over?

April 1940 • Like

Winston Churchill > Neville Chamberlain Alright GTFO.

May 10, 1940 • Comment • Like

British Parliament Seriously.

May 10, 1940 • Like

Adolf Hitler > Winston Churchill What happened to that Chamberlain guy? And who are you?

May 10, 1940 • Comment • Like

Winston Churchill I'm Winston Fucking Churchill.

May 10, 1940 • Like

Britain Reguuulatooooors, MOUNT UP.

May 10, 1940 • Like

Germany created an event.

The Blitz

London Bridge is falling down, falling down, falling down!

31 September 7, 1940 • Comment • Like • Share • RSVP to this event

Britain

September 7, 1940 • Comment • Like

United States You guys all cool over there?
September 7, 1940 • Like

Britain Oh yeah, fine. Just a bunch of hearts and sparkles. Can't you tell from the pic?
September 7, 1940 • Like

United States Is that sarcasm?
September 7, 1940 • Like

Britain YES. HELP.
September 7, 1940 • Like

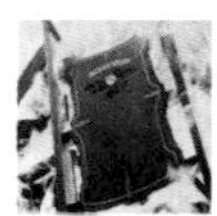

Charles Foster Kane Spoiler alert: it's my sled.
May 1, 1941 • Comment • Like

Adolf Hitler > Joseph Stalin Sorry things didn't work out, Joe, but you leave me no choice. Gonna have to kick your ass across the Russian tundra. There's no stopping me now.
July 3, 1941 • Comment • Like

Napoleon Bonaparte Not a student of history, Adolf?
July 3, 1941 • Like

Ilsa Lund Going to the local gin joint for a nightcap... Rick's Café Americain.
December 3, 1941 • Comment • Like

Rick Blaine You have GOT to be kidding me.
December 3, 1941 • Like

Japan has created the event **Bomb Party in Pearl Harbor!**.
31 December 6, 1941 • Comment • Like • Share • RSVP to this event

America Wait, what?
December 6, 1941 • Like

Japan Oh I mean it's gonna be "tha bomb"... as in, really fun.
December 6, 1941 • Like

America Ah, ok. Thought you meant something else.
December 6, 1941 • Like

Japan has made the event **Bomb Party in Pearl Harbor!** private.
31 December 6, 1941 • Comment • Like • Share • RSVP to this event

---

Japan — checked in to **Pearl Harbor**.
December 7, 1941 • Comment • Like

Infamy likes this.

The United States You made me angry.
December 7, 1941 • Like

Japan So?
December 7, 1941 • Like

The United States You're not going to like me when I'm angry.
December 7, 1941 • Like

The United States is attending **World War II**.
December 7, 1941 • Comment • Like

The United States is in a domestic partnership with **The Allies**.
December 7, 1941 • Comment • Like

Britain About time, mate.
December 7, 1941 • Like

France We surrender!
December 7, 1941 • Like

Britain Same team.
December 7, 1941 • Like

France Ah.
December 7, 1941 • Like

Rosie the Riveter

Female Workforce Efficient, Productive in Factories
Nation "Surprised" by Performance Outside Kitchen

January 21, 1942 • Comment • Like

Sexism These are sandwich factories, right?
January 21, 1942 • Like

President Franklin D. Roosevelt likes **Executive Order 9066**.
February 19, 1942 • Comment • Like

Racism likes this.

President Franklin D. Roosevelt > Japanese-Americans
You guys want to go camping?
February 19, 1942 • Comment • Like

Japanese-Americans This weekend? Sure. Whereabouts?
February 19, 1942 • Like

President Roosevelt Great new spot: Internment National Park. And actually it'll be more of an extended weekend. Very extended.
February 19, 1942 • Like

U.S. Marines Keep the sand out of your weapons. Keep those actions clear. I'll see you on the beach.
June 6, 1942 • Comment • Like

Tom Hanks really, really likes this.

Germany oh balls
June 6, 1942 • Like

France I can surrender again if that helps.
June 6, 1942 • Like

Enrico Fermi

Top Physicists Head to New Mexico for "Team-Building Retreat"
Scientists Participating in Trust Falls, Name Games, "Nothing Serious, Promise"

June 8, 1942 • Comment • Like

J. Robert Oppenheimer likes this.

Japan lol you guys are just wasting your time over there.
June 8, 1942 • Like

Enrico Fermi Why, yes. Yes, we are.
June 8, 1942 • Like

Howard Hughes

Howard Hughes Building World's Largest Plane
Wartime Rationing Requires Construction of Only Wood, Mania, Ego

June 8, 1942 • Comment • Like

Howard Hughes Show me all the blueprints. Show me all the blueprints. Show me all the blueprints.
June 8, 1942 • Like

Anne Frank OK this is a *really* intense game of Hide and Seek.
July 6, 1942 • Comment • Like

Kitty likes this.

American Jews > European Jews How you guys holding up over there? Haven't heard from you in a while.

July 6, 1942 • Comment • Like

American Jews Hello?

July 6, 1942 • Like

The British Air Force tagged **Hamburg, Germany** in a video.

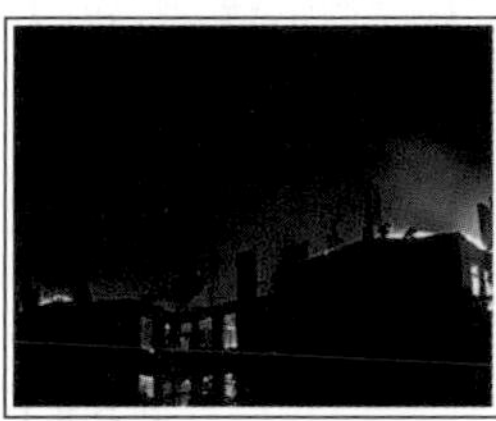

July 6, 1942 • Comment • Like

Fire likes this.

Auschwitz Remember, work makes you free!

July 6, 1942 • Comment • Like

United States > Germany SUP.

July 6, 1942 • Comment • Like

France likes this.

Britain lol

July 6, 1942 • Like

Joe Rosenthal — is on **Iwo Jima** with **U.S. Marines**.

February 23, 1945 • Comment • Like

Joe Rosenthal > U.S. Marines Fellas, grab that flag and let me take a picture.
February 23, 1945 • Comment • Like

U.S. Marines Cheeeeese
February 23, 1945 • Like

Joe Rosenthal Not bad.

February 23, 1945 • Comment • Like

The United States LOVES this.

Clint Eastwood fap fap fap
February 23, 1945 • Like

New York Times

VICTORY IN EUROPE:
Hitler Commits Suicide, Nazis Surrender!
Argentina Notices Large Influx of German "Tourists"

April 20, 1945 • Comment • Like

Japan Whatever, I'm fine rolling solo. Bring it. Not surrendering.
April 20, 1945 • Like

The Enola Gay — is in **Hiroshima** with **Little Boy**.
August 7, 1945 • Comment • Like

Japan Little who?
August 7, 1945 • Like

The United States

August 9, 1945 • Comment • Like

Nobody likes this.

Japan o_O
August 9, 1945 • Like

Japan created an event.

Surrendering!
Forget what I said earlier.

August 9, 1945 • Comment • Like • Share • RSVP to this event

USS Missouri PEACE
August 9, 1945 • Like

The United States

With War Over, Entire Nation Focuses on Having Sex
Obstetricians Plan to Finally Buy Condo in Boca Raton

August 9, 1945 • Comment • Like

New York Times

United Nations Created
Will Write Stern Letters, Offer College Internships, Not Much Else

October 24, 1945 • Comment • Like

Chuck Yeager — is at **The Sound Barrier** with **Glamorous Glennis**.

December 1947 • Comment • Like

Chuck Yeager holyshiiiiiiiiiiiiiiiiiiiiiiiiiiiiiiiiiiiiiiiiiiiiiiiiiiiiiiiiiii

December 1947 • Like

Soviet Union Giving **West Berlin** a big, warm Communist hug.

June 24, 1948 • Comment • Like

West Berlin Um, this is more of a big, warm blockade.

June 24, 1948 • Like

Soviet Union Tomato tomahto.

June 24, 1948 • Like

West Berlin We're doomed. Wait, look! It's a bird... It's a plane! IT'S...

June 24, 1948 • Comment • Like

Democracy likes this.

The United States Just a plane. I thought you could use some goodies.
June 24, 1948 • Like

West Berlin Yaaay
June 24, 1948 • Like

Soviet Union And I would've gotten away with it too if it weren't for you meddling kids!
June 24, 1948 • Like

The New York Yankees

Babe Ruth Dead at 53
Immortalized in Hall of Fame, on Delicious Candy Bar

August 16, 1948 • Comment • Like

The '50s added Consuming to its Interests.
December 1949 • Comment • Like

New York Times Book Review > L. Ron Hubbard
Read your book. What an achievement. Such a fantastic parody of the crazed cult mentality.
May 9, 1950 • Comment • Like

L. Ron Hubbard Parody?
May 9, 1950 • Like

Jackson Pollock Dammit. Spilled my paints all over a new canvas.
May 9, 1950 • Comment • Like

Jackson Pollock Actually doesn't look bad.
May 9, 1950 • Like

Holden Caulfield Goddamn statuses. I can't stand them. It's just another lousy way for people to feel important, which is all life is really, if you think about it, just a bunch of phonies wanting to be important for cryin' out loud.
August 12, 1951 • Comment • Like

Danny Zuko This puppy really flies!

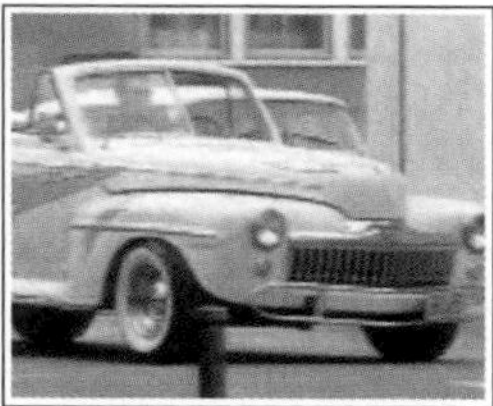

September 9, 1952 • Comment • Like

Sandra Dee likes this.

Kenickie Ha, when I first read that I thought you meant actual flying, like driving up into the clouds!
September 9, 1952 • Like

Danny Zuko ...
September 9, 1952 • Like

Ian Fleming Need a good name for my novel's protagonist: a cunning British spy, attractive, and the definition of cool. Suggestions?
April 13, 1953 • Comment • Like

MI6 Jerry Frond.
April 13, 1953 • Like

Ian Fleming Not sexy enough. Or at all, really.
April 13, 1953 • Like

MI6 James Bondowski.
April 13, 1953 • Like

Ian Fleming He doesn't drive a forklift.
April 13, 1953 • Like

MI6 Jamesh Bhondi?
April 13, 1953 • Like

Ian Fleming Or a taxi.
April 13, 1953 • Like

Sir Edmund Hillary — is on **Mt. Everest** with **Tenzing Norgay**.
May 29, 1953 • Comment • Like

London Times

Everest Summited! Edmund Hillary to Become a Household Name
Foreign Companion, Not So Much

May 30, 1953 • Comment • Like

Death > Internal Revenue Service I hear you're pretty reliable.
July 9, 1953 • Comment • Like

Edward R. Murrow Don't listen to political gasbags who try and scare you with falsehoods and thinly veiled propaganda.
March 9, 1954 • Comment • Like

Joseph McCarthy Who you callin' a gasbag?
March 9, 1954 • Like

Fox News Yeah?!
March 9, 1954 • Like

James Dean Got myself a new little Porsche.
March 9, 1954 • Comment • Like

Rolf Wütherich Fast?
March 9, 1954 • Like

James Dean Yep.
March 9, 1954 • Like

Rolf Wütherich Safe?
March 9, 1954 • Like

James Dean Eh.
March 9, 1954 • Like

Vladimir Nabokov added **Sex with Underage Girls** to his Interests.
September 15, 1955 • Comment • Like

Vladimir Nabokov That looks bad, but I swear it's for research.
September 15, 1955 • Like

Doctor Emmett Brown Learned something today: don't stand on your toilet to hang a clock. It's unsafe. Also, time travel is possible.
November 5, 1955 • Comment • Like

Marty McFly Where the hell?...
November 5, 1955 • Like

Lorraine Baines hey cutie ;-)
November 5, 1955 • Like

Marty McFly Oh no.
November 5, 1955 • Like

Rosa Parks Bad day at work, my feet are killing me, all I want to do is sit down and not be bothered. Not in the mood for bullshit.
December 1, 1955 • Comment • Like

Norma Jeane Mortenson changed her name to **Marilyn Monroe.**
February 23, 1956 • Comment • Like

Joe DiMaggio and **18 million other men** like this.

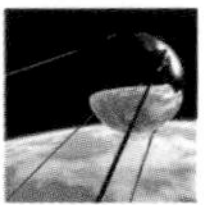

Sputnik > Soviet Union 01100010 01100101
October 4, 1957 • Comment • Like

Soviet Union likes this.

The United States Oh no.
October 4, 1957 • Like

IBM

IBM Builds Computer Machine in Airplane Hangar
Does Basic Arithmetic, Occasionally Beeps

1957 • Comment • Like

IBM The amazing thing? Someday a computer like this will be able to fit into a single room.
1957 • Like

Texas Instruments Waste of time. The future is calculators.
1957 • Like

The United States

Alaska Becomes State
Provides Nation with Bear Supply, Ability to See Soviets from Backyard

July 7, 1958 • Comment • Like

Buddy Holly Couple extra seats on this plane, anyone want 'em?
February 3, 1959 • Comment • Like

Fate likes this.

Big Bopper I'll take one.
February 3, 1959 • Like

Ritchie Valens Me too!
February 3, 1959 • Like

Don McLean — is at **The Levee** with his **Chevy**.
February 3, 1959 • Comment • Like

Good Ol' Boy Whiskey? Rye?
February 3, 1959 • Like

Joseph McNeil was tagged in **Franklin McCain**'s album.

Woolworth's Lunch Counter

February 1, 1960 • Comment • Like

Martin Luther King Jr. likes this.

Ku Klux Klan UGH LAME
February 1, 1960 • Like

John Lennon is now friends with **Paul McCartney** and **2 others**.

March 5, 1960 • Comment • Like

Girls OMG
March 5, 1960 • Like

Food and Drug Administration just decided that this "birth control" pill is alright by me.
May 9, 1960 • Comment • Like

Women WOOHOO
May 9, 1960 • Like

Yuri Gagarin — checked in to **Orbit**.
April 12, 1961 • Comment • Like

Soviet Union F1rst!
April 12, 1961 • Like

The United States Double or nothing: the moon.
April 12, 1961 • Like

Soviet Union You're on.
April 12, 1961 • Like

NASA The WHAT?!
April 12, 1961 • Like

John F. Kennedy Just... make it so.
April 12, 1961 • Like

Ted Kennedy > John F. Kennedy Happy B-day, bro.
May 29, 1962 • Comment • Like

Robert Kennedy > John F. Kennedy Happy birthday, Johnny.
May 29, 1962 • Comment • Like

Marilyn Monroe > John F. Kennedy Haaappy Birthdaaaay, Mr. Preeeesident.
May 29, 1962 • Comment • Like

Jackie Kennedy Step off, hussy.
May 29, 1962 • Like

Frank Morris — is somewhere in the **San Francisco Bay** with **John Anglin** and **Clarence Anglin**.

June 11, 1962 • Comment • Like

Alcatraz Prison !!!!

June 11, 1962 • Like

Frank Morris Get busy livin, or get busy dyin'.

June 11, 1962 • Like

Communism > Vietnam I'm heading down to SE Asia, you around?

June 11, 1962 • Comment • Like

Vietnam Yep!

June 11, 1962 • Like

Soviet Union Nice.

June 11, 1962 • Like

US Military GAME TIME.

June 11, 1962 • Like

Soviet Union was tagged in **U2**'s album.

Snaps from My Flaps

November 20, 1962 • Comment • Like

John F. Kennedy Are those missile silos?

November 20, 1962 • Like

Premier Khrushchev Wha? Noooo!

November 20, 1962 • Like

Fidel Castro Khrushie, the silos are ready.

November 20, 1962 • Like

Fidel Castro oh. oops.

November 20, 1962 • Like

United States NOT COOL.

Soviets Put Nukes on Cuba
Game of High-Stakes Chicken Ensues, Nation Heads into Their Basements

November 20, 1962 • Comment • Like

President John F. Kennedy > Premier Khrushchev I have a big red button that you don't want me to push.
November 20, 1962 • Comment • Like

Premier Khrushchev Funny thing--I have one too.
November 20, 1962 • Like

Mutually Assured Destruction I like where this is headed!
November 20, 1962 • Like

Earth CHILL, GUYS
November 20, 1962 • Like

John F. Kennedy Beautiful day in Dallas! Gonna get all presidential up in here and drop the top.
November 22, 1963 • Comment • Like

Lee Harvey Oswald likes this.

Jack Ruby WAIT
November 22, 1963 • Like

Lyndon Johnson likes the **Civil Rights Act of 1964.**
July 2, 1964 • Comment • Like

Alabama When are we getting that "dislike" button?
July 2, 1964 • Like

Mississippi Seriously.
July 2, 1964 • Like

Arkansas Ugh.
July 2, 1964 • Like

Lyndon Johnson

Incident in Gulf of Tonkin
Totally Real Event,
Not Made Up, Promise

August 2, 1964 • Comment • Like

American Public Oh no!
August 2, 1964 • Like

Lyndon Johnson Oh yes, it's true. Cross my fingers. I mean my heart.
August 2, 1964 • Like

Lyndon Johnson created the event Small Altercation in Vietnam.
1965 • Comment • Like • Share • RSVP to this event

Lyndon Johnson Over in a few weeks, tops.
1965 • Like

Iraq Totally.
1965 • Like

Martin Luther King Jr. Great view! — at **The Mountaintop**.
1967 • Comment • Like

Martin Luther King Jr. added **The Promised Land** to his Interests.
1967 • Comment • Like

Che Guevara Captured. Got a date with a firing squad. Doesn't look good for the Che-meister.
October 7, 1967 • Comment • Like

Fulgencio Batista Hope you enjoy perforations!
October 7, 1967 • Like

Che Guevara Whatever. I shall leave my mark on history.

October 7, 1967 • Like

Fulgencio Batista If by "history" you mean countless t-shirts and stoner posters, then yes, you certainly will.

October 7, 1967 • Like

Che Guevara Just kill me now.

October 7, 1967 • Like

Dave Bowman > HAL 9000 Little help with these pod bay doors, Hal?

1968 • Comment • Like

Dave Bowman Hal?

1968 • Like

Johnny Cash

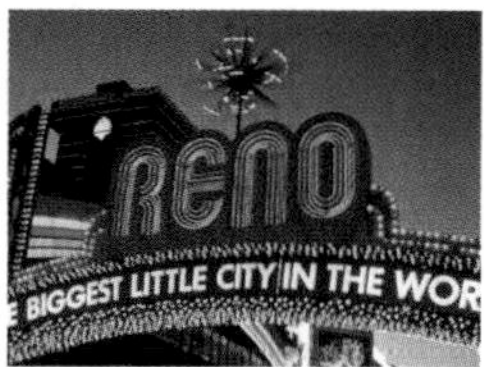

Reno Man Shot, Motive Unclear
Witnesses Say Gunman Just "Watched Victim Die"

February 24, 1969 • Comment • Like

Saturn V Alright let's do this... LEROOOOY JENKINNNNNS

July 21, 1969 • Comment • Like

Neil Armstrong ahhhhhhhh

July 21, 1969 • Like

Buzz Aldrin ahhhhhhhhh

July 21, 1969 • Like

Michael Collins ahhhhhh
July 21, 1969 • Like

Neil Armstrong — is on **The Moon** with **Buzz Aldrin**.
July 21, 1969 • Comment • Like

John F. Kennedy would've liked this.

The United States Epic.
July 21, 1969 • Like

Neil Armstrong That's one small step for man, one gonad swap for manatee.
July 21, 1969 • Comment • Like

Neil Armstrong Dammit autocorrect.
July 21, 1969 • Like

NASA One for the history books, Neil.
July 21, 1969 • Like

Benjamin Braddock is now friends with **Mrs. Robinson**.

July 21, 1969 • Comment • Like

Simon and Garfunkel like this.

Neil Armstrong Honestly it feels like I'm walking on a giant powdered donut, but it's the MOON.

July 21, 1969 • Comment • Like

Apollo 13 Can't wait for our turn!
July 21, 1969 • Like

American Youth created an event.

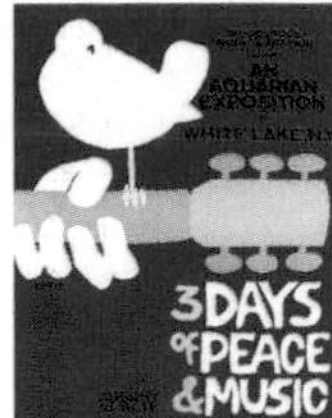

Celebrate Peace with Music, Love, and Some Really Great Drugs.
Contact Daisy Sunshine Rainbowflower for details.

August 18, 1969 • Comment • Like • Share • RSVP to this event

Richard Nixon Wow, you're right. I must give peace a chance: I'm calling the whole war off.
August 18, 1969 • Like

American Youth Really!?
August 18, 1969 • Like

Richard Nixon No. Go dance in circles.
August 18, 1969 • Like

Lyndon Johnson created the event The Draft.
August 18, 1969 • Comment • Like • Share • RSVP to this event

Lyndon Johnson Don't burn that little card, fellas, you may need it!
August 18, 1969 • Like

American Youth This aggression will not stand, man.
August 18, 1969 • Like

Lieutenant Colonel Bill Kilgore Smells nice.

Military Introduces Napalm Strikes Against Vietcong

August 18, 1969 • Comment • Like

Richard Nixon We're winning the Extended Small Altercation in Vietnam.
August 18, 1969 • Comment • Like

Vietnamese Civilian That title is an Extended Small Fabrication.
August 18, 1969 • Like

North Vietnam lol
August 18, 1969 • Like

Richard Nixon Oh look, just ordered more bombs.
August 18, 1969 • Like

The Washington Post

The Washington Post

Richard Nixon Is a Crook!

August 18, 1969 • Comment • Like

Bob Woodward likes this.

Richard Nixon AM NOT
August 18, 1969 • Like

Richard Nixon is no longer in a relationship with **The United States.**
August 18, 1969 • Comment • Like

David Frost You want to talk about it?
August 18, 1969 • Like

Gerald Ford Aaaand scene. Peace out, Vietnam, pardon the pun.
August 18, 1969 • Comment • Like

North Vietnam See you soon, Saigon.
August 18, 1969 • Like

Saigon Uh, Gerald, hang on a sec, I could use some help here.
August 18, 1969 • Like

Gerald Ford Sorry, dude. Got tickets to Creedence tonight.
August 18, 1969 • Like

Saigon But...
August 18, 1969 • Like

Gerald Ford I'mnotlisteningLALALALA
August 18, 1969 • Like

North Vietnam > Saigon Knock knock...
August 18, 1969 • Comment • Like

Saigon Who's there?
August 18, 1969 • Like

North Vietnam Me. Like, right now.
August 18, 1969 • Like

Saigon -sigh-
August 18, 1969 • Like

George Lucas > Steven Spielberg What about this--an epic good vs. evil story, maybe like a classic western, but in SPACE.
April 2, 1977 • Comment • Like

Steven Spielberg Like on the moon?
April 2, 1977 • Like

George Lucas No, no, like a long time ago, in a galaxy far far away.
April 2, 1977 • Like

Steven Spielberg Dunno. Sounds a little ambitious.
April 2, 1977 • Like

George Lucas Really?! I find your lack of faith disturbing.
April 2, 1977 • Like

Tony Manero is in a relationship with **Disco**.
December 14, 1977 • Comment • Like

The Bee Gees like this.

Idi Amin Having my esteemed Minister of the Interior for dinner.
August 11, 1978 • Comment • Like

Idi Amin *over* for dinner.
August 11, 1978 • Like

Information Age

In the middle of the twentieth century, humanity witnessed a breakthrough in electronic technology. The invention of the microprocessor and the personal computer revolutionized our world. With technology advancing at a near exponential rate, instant digital communication across vast distances became possible.

A few decades later, millions of independent computers and their users began connecting with one another, forming the most extensive and accessible communication network in human history: the Internet. The Internet became a global hive mind, a digital library of endless information, and any connected individual anywhere in the world could tap into this vast compendium of pornography and cat videos. Humanity rejoiced.

Moreover, individuals across the globe could actively contribute to this "Internet" by sharing important facts from their own lives—such as a picture of the salad they ate for lunch—or by participating in forums for cyclical political bickering, or by simply posting homophobic comments using all capital letters and stroke-victim spelling. Deposed Nigerian princes, who for decades had been unable to send their besieged fortunes to trustworthy foreign partners, suddenly could reach out to distant strangers with "a request for kind and expedient assistanting of confident fund transference." The future was bright indeed.

The '70s and **Cocaine** — are at **Studio 54** with **Bianca Jagger** and **Andy Warhol**.

July 7, 1979 • Comment • Like

Steve Rubell likes this.

The '80s Dude! Dudedudedude. I'm so jazzed right now. This club is off the chain! We need more champagne, because this stuff is like, the best fucking champagne I've HEY WAITRESS, we'll just get two bottles because the night is still young WAITRESS, HELLO, hold up look at those girls. They're like models and... wait... you're friends with them?! Man, you are pals with EVERYONE around here! Except the fucking waitress who is icing me hard right now. Hey you heard the new Huey Lewis? Their early work was a little too New Wave for my tastes, but when "Sports" came out in '83, I think they really came into their own, commercially and artistically. Wow. My vision is, like, vibrating. I need some water. I'm sweating and my teeth hurt.

July 7, 1979 • Like

The '80s is in a relationship with **Bad Taste**.

April 4, 1980 • Comment • Like

Stirrup Pants, **Mullets**, and **Synth** like this.

Michael Jackson You still got me.

April 4, 1980 • Like

Madonna Me too.

April 4, 1980 • Like

Hall & Oates We're here if you need to talk.

April 4, 1980 • Like

Ghost > Pac-Man C'mere.

May 22, 1980 • Comment • Like

Pac-Man is now friends with **Power Pellet**.

May 22, 1980 • Comment • Like

Ghost changed its profile picture.
May 22, 1980 • Comment • Like

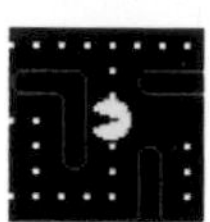

Pac-Man > **Ghost** C'mere.
May 22, 1980 • Comment • Like

The '80s is now friends with **Personal Computers** and **Compact Discs**.

May 22, 1980 • Comment • Like

Typewriters fuuuuu
May 22, 1980 • Like

Tape Cassettes Oh no.
May 22, 1980 • Like

8-Track JUSTICE.
May 22, 1980 • Like

Princess Peach — is at **Another Castle** with **King Koopa**.
1983 • Comment • Like

Mario you've got to be kidding me.
1983 • Like

The '80s is now friends with **Cell Phones**.

1983 • Comment • Like

Land Lines This decade blows.
1983 • Like

Answering Machines Totally.
1983 • Like

Sarah Connor is now friends with **Kyle Reese**.

April 26, 1984 • Comment • Like

Fate likes this.

Guess Jeans

New Acid-Based Denim Treatment to Revolutionize Fashion

April 26, 1984 • Comment • Like

Whitesnake likes this.

The '80s and **Excess** are now friends.

April 26, 1984 • Comment • Like

Bret Easton Ellis and **Gordon Gekko** like this.

Sarah Conner — checked in to the **West Highland Police Station** with **Kyle Reese**.
1984 • Comment • Like

Diego Maradona > **God** Just wanted to say thanks for lending a hand on that goal.
1984 • Comment • Like

God All you, baby.
1984 • Like

Chernobyl Power Plant Running a quick test on the ol' reactoooooh SHIT
April 26, 1986 • Comment • Like

Murphy's Law likes this.

Soviet Union Everything is fine. Nothing is wrong. I got this. I mean, if there was a "this." Which there isn't.
April 26, 1986 • Like

Lacoste

Collar Epidemic Sweeps Nation
Preppy Clothing Executives Toast Arrival of "The Douchebag"

December 1986 • Comment • Like

Patrick Bateman — is at **Dorsia**.
December 1986 • Comment • Like

Patrick Bateman likes this.

ESPRIT

Fall Fashion:
Stylish Cure for Cold Legs?

December 1986 • Comment • Like

Michael Jackson concert starts in 6 minutes, and I can't find my other white glove.
February 19, 1987 • Comment • Like

Michael Jackson or my damn black socks!
February 19, 1987 • Like

The Proclaimers

Man Declares He'd Walk
500 Miles for Girl
Possibly Walk 500 More

August 15, 1988 • Comment • Like

Exxon Valdez Partying in Alaska. There's this girl here tryin to convince me you can see Russia from her house. Handle your booze, girl.
March 24, 1989 • Comment • Like

Exxon Valdez omg I think something hit us. this is totes killing my buzz.
March 24, 1989 • Like

Environmental Protection Agency Beg your pardon?
March 24, 1989 • Like

Exxon Valdez Oh wow, that's a lot of oil.
March 24, 1989 • Like

Environmental Protection Agency WHAT
March 24, 1989 • Like

BP lol would hate to be you
March 24, 1989 • Like

Bird FML
March 24, 1989 • Comment • Like

Exxon Valdez Oh whatever you look way better in black anyway.
March 24, 1989 • Like

China

Brave Homeless Man Offers to Wash Tank Windshields
Amazing Display of the Human Spirit, Annoying Extortion

June 4, 1989 • Comment • Like

East Germany Sorry, everyone, the party's over.
November 9, 1989 • Comment • Like

Democracy and Capitalism like this.

Berlin Wall Whoa whoa whoa.... wtf is this?
November 9, 1989 • Like

Socialist Unity Party No, he's right. I'm toast.
November 9, 1989 • Like

Berlin Wall Well this is just fantastic. I'm going to get smashed apart.
November 9, 1989 • Like

Kool-Aid OH YEAH!
November 9, 1989 • Like

New York Times

Researchers Create "World Wide Web" of Electronic Communication
This Might Be Kind of a Big Deal

August 6, 1991 • Comment • Like

Porn likes this.

Sir Mix-a-Lot added Big Butts and Not Lying to his Interests.
May 7, 1992 • Comment • Like

MTV is now friends with **Reality Television**.

May 21, 1992 • Comment • Like

Viewers This won't take away from the music programming, right?
May 21, 1992 • Like

MTV Psh. Of course not.
May 21, 1992 • Like

Nancy Kerrigan OW MY KNEE
January 6, 1994 • Comment • Like

Tonya Harding likes this.

Sony PlayStation

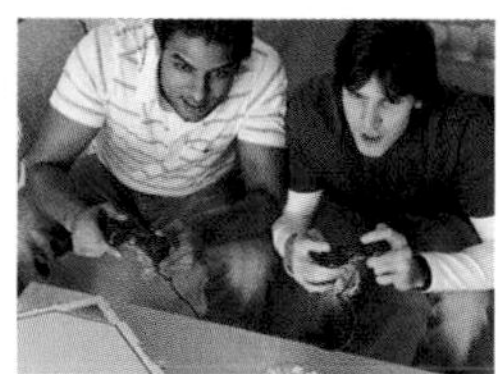

Video Game Sales See Meteoric Rise Strangely, So Does Male Virginity

December 4, 1994 • Comment • Like

Hollywood is now friends with **DVDs**.

September 5, 1995 • Comment • Like

Bootleggers like this.

VHS But rewinding is fun!
September 5, 1995 • Like

O. J. Simpson

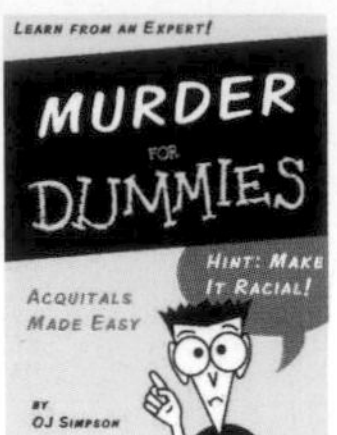

Getting Away with Murder for Dummies
10 Easy Steps to Turn a Sure Conviction into a Race-Baiting Media-Clusterfucking Acquittal!

October 3, 1995 • Comment • Like

Johnnie Cochran likes this.

Lady Justice Fail.
October 3, 1995 • Like

Ted Kaczynski changed his profile picture.
October 3, 1995 • Comment • Like

Woody is now friends with **Buzz Lightyear** and **5 others**.

November 22, 1995 • Comment • Like

CGI likes this.

IBM's "Deep Blue" > Garry Kasparov That's checkmate, human.
February 10, 1996 • Comment • Like

Cyberdyne Systems likes this.

Comet Hale-Bopp > Earth What up? Been a while!
March 23, 1997 • Comment • Like

Heaven's Gate Cult That's our cue.
March 23, 1997 • Like

U.S. Postal Service > America Online Look, I appreciate your business, but I'm not sure another 18 million CDs is going to help.
June 10, 1997 • Comment • Like

Evander Holyfield is no longer in a relationship with **His Ear**.
June 28, 1997 • Comment • Like

Mike Tyson likes this.

Skynet Waaaait a sec... I'm a computer, aren't I?
August 29, 1997 • Comment • Like

The Pentagon Shit.
August 29, 1997 • Like

Paula Jones > Monica Lewinsky Look on the bright side; you have something new to add to your resume.
January 26, 1998 • Comment • Like

Monica Lewinsky That's a low blow.
January 26, 1998 • Like

Paula Jones Precisely.
January 26, 1998 • Like

Lance Armstrong is in a relationship with **Cancer**.
1998 • Comment • Like

Lance Armstrong is listed as separated from his... yeah, that.
1998 • Comment • Like

Google added **Internet Search** to its Interests.
September 4, 1998 • Comment • Like

Metacrawler Awful big pond for you, little fishy
September 4, 1998 • Like

Lycos lol
September 4, 1998 • Like

Altavista welcome to the Majors, kiddo
September 4, 1998 • Like

Hotbot Destined to fail
September 4, 1998 • Like

Lance Armstrong is no longer in a relationship with **Cancer.**
1999 • Comment • Like

Thomas Anderson Whoa.
1999 • Comment • Like

Morpheus likes this

The Internet is now friends with **Napster.**

June 15, 1999 • Comment • Like

RIAA Nooooo
June 15, 1999 • Like

Voters Screw policy, I'm going to vote for the guy who has trouble forming sentences.
November 6, 2000 • Comment • Like

George W. Bush likes this.

The United States I'm sure it'll play out well.
November 6, 2000 • Like

Jimmy Wales is now in a relationship with **Wikipedia.**
January 15, 2001 • Comment • Like

High School Students Yesssss
January 15, 2001 • Like

Microsoft Encarta Noooooo
January 15, 2001 • Like

Enron Let's see... carry the 4... yep, we have a 8 bazillion dollars in the bank.
August 18, 2001 • Comment • Like

Kenneth Lay and **WorldCom** like this.

Securties and Exchange Commission Sorry, how much?
August 18, 2001 • Like

Enron 8 um, gazillions.
August 18, 2001 • Like

Securities and Exchange Commission Can I see your accounting books?
August 18, 2001 • Like

Enron Oh look, a pretty bird!
August 18, 2001 • Like

Osama Bin Laden About to become a household name in 3...2...
September 10, 2001 • Comment • Like

Nobody forgets this.

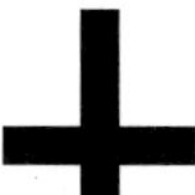

Satan > 9/11 Hijackers I know what you're thinking... where those 40 virgins at, right? Two words for ya, fellas: False. Advertising. Welcome though, so glad you're here. #ohsnap
September 11, 2001 • Comment • Like

The Twin Towers It's a tragedy. So let's not evoke this day to mindlessly push a belligerent political agenda, k?
September 11, 2001 • Comment • Like

2,977 people like this.

Apple iPod Hello, world!
October 23, 2001 • Comment • Like

Steve Jobs and **600 million people** like this.

Microsoft iPod!?
October 23, 2001 • Like

Bernie Madoff is now friends with **Charles Ponzi**.

October 23, 2001 • Comment • Like

Wall Street likes this.

Mark Zuckerberg Got an idea.
2003 • Comment • Like

Winklevoss Twins Our idea?
2003 • Like

President George W. Bush is in a relationship with **Iraqi WMDs**, and it's contrived.
January 8, 2003 • Comment • Like

Halliburton likes this.

Dick Cheney Exxxxxcellent.
January 8, 2003 • Like

Space Shuttle Columbia Descending into the atmosphere after a successful mission. Put the champagne on ice, NASA, we're coming ho
February 1, 2003 • Comment • Like

Heroism likes this.

Houston Mission Control Guys? Hello?
February 1, 2003 • Like

President George W. Bush YEEHAW

U.S. Declares War on Iraq
Public Opinion: "Them Iraqis Look Just Like the Terrorists!"

March 20, 2003 • Comment • Like

The Twin Towers -sigh-
March 20, 2003 • Like

Iraq > The United States WTF did I do?!
March 20, 2003 • Comment • Like

Dick Cheney You have Weapons of Oil Production.
March 20, 2003 • Like

Dick Cheney I mean Weapons of Mass Petroleum.
March 20, 2003 • Like

Dr. Sigmund Freud Stop. Just stop.
March 20, 2003 • Like

Dick Cheney GIVES ME MY PRECIOUS
March 20, 2003 • Like

Dick Cheney added **Puppeteering** to his Interests.
March 30, 2003 • Comment • Like

President George W. Bush This will be over in a month or two, tops.
April 10, 2003 • Comment • Like

Donald Rumsfeld likes this.

Vietnam Though heavy, history books are often worth picking up.
April 10, 2003 • Like

President George W. Bush Shock and Awed, baby!

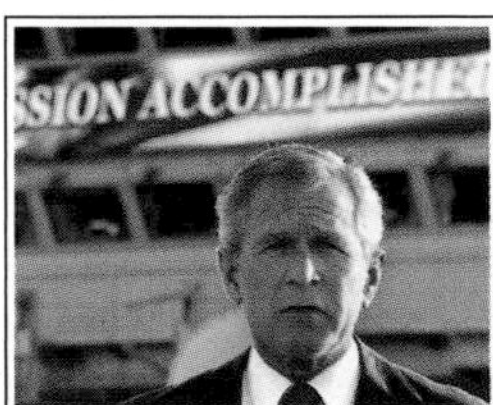

May 1, 2003 • Comment • Like

Irony likes this.

SARS > **China** BOO!
November 20, 2003 • Comment • Like

China AHH!
November 20, 2003 • Like

SARS lol
November 20, 2003 • Like

Saddam Hussein Chilling — in my **Spider Hole.**
December 13, 2003 • Comment • Like

U.S. Marines Wow, thanks.
December 13, 2003 • Like

Saddam Hussein shit.
December 13, 2003 • Like

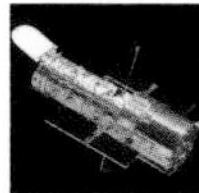

Hubble Space Telescope

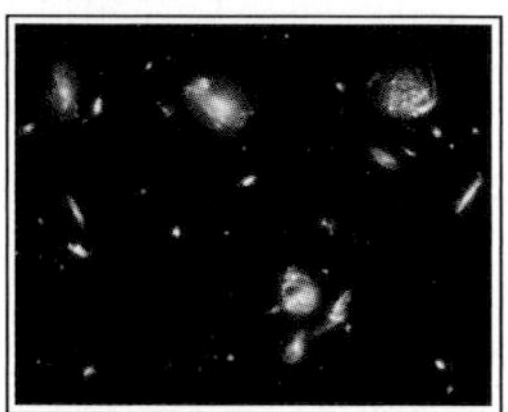

January 16, 2004 • Comment • Like

Humility likes this.

Humans Those thousands of stars?
January 16, 2004 • Like

NASA No. Galaxies.
January 16, 2004 • Like

Humans o_O
January 16, 2004 • Like

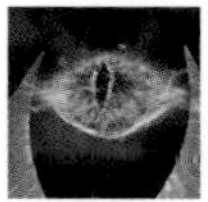

Sauron > Dick Cheney Really admire your work.
April 19, 2004 • Comment • Like

Dick Cheney likes this.

Dick Cheney is now friends with **Darth Sidious** and **Mr. Burns.**

May 15, 2004 • Comment • Like

Auto-Tune > Talent I'm sorry to be the bearer of bad news, but your services are no longer required.
June 9, 2004 • Comment • Like

Black Eyed Peas like this.

Jay-Z -sigh-
June 9, 2004 • Like

Boston Red Sox > New York Yankees HOW DYA LIKE DEM APPLES
October 27, 2004 • Comment • Like

Will Hunting likes this.

Tectonic Plates Hey all, I'm moving to a new place on the 26th. Just wanted to give people the heads up. Especially **Indonesia, Thailand, India,** and **Sri Lanka.**
December 24, 2004 • Comment • Like

Lance Armstrong

Lance Armstrong Wins
7th Tour de France
At This Point He's Almost
Assuredly a Robot

July 24, 2005 • Comment • Like

Hurricane Katrina > New Orleans Great tune, amiright?!

When the Levee Breaks — Led Zeppelin

August 25, 2005 • Comment • Like

FEMA likes this, and did shit about it.

New Orleans Not... really.
August 25, 2005 • Like

Planet Earth Is it just me or does it feel a little warm in here?
July 9, 2006 • Comment • Like

Al Gore likes this. Kind of.

Exxon Mobil LALALALA NOT LISTENING
July 9, 2006 • Like

Republicans lol whatevs
July 9, 2006 • Like

Zinedine Zindane Header!

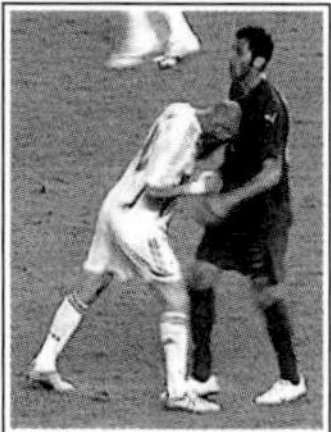

2006 • Comment • Like

Italy likes this.

France Zanks for loosing ze game for us.
2006 • Like

Captain Falcon Next time go with the PUUUUNCH
2006 • Like

Barbaro Smoked 'em at the Kentucky Derby and now gonna smoke 'em at the PreakneOWWWW
2006 • Comment • Like

Steve Jobs Ladies and gentlemen, the iPhone.

Apple Reveals Amazing Long-Awaited iPhone
Verizon Executives Curse Under Breath, Kick Dog

2007 • Comment • Like

Buttons Noooooooooo
2007 • Like

Michael Bay added **Robots** to his Interests.
2007 • Comment • Like

Hasbro likes this.

Barry Bonds 756!
2007 • Comment • Like

Baseball Hall of Fame 756*
2007 • Like

New York Giants > New England Patriots

Choke

(chok) v. — 1. To interfere with respiration by the compression or obstruction of the larynx or trachea. 2. To fail to perform effectively in crucial moments. 3. 18-1.

2008 • Comment • Like

John McCain "Yes We Can?" Psh. Sounds like a tagline for Cialis.
2008 • Comment • Like

Barack Obama You would know...
2008 • Like

Sarah Palin herp derp i readz all the newspapers!
2008 • Comment • Like

Barack Obama likes this.

John McCain Hey let's play the quiet game, k?
2008 • Like

Sarah Palin I CAN SEE RUSSIA
2008 • Like

John McCain I've made a huuuuge mistake.
2008 • Like

The New York Times

Barack Obama Elected President
Nation Rejoices, If Only Because Bush Is Finally Out

2008 • Comment • Like

Equality likes this.

Europe Sorry, everyone, flights are cancelled because of that volcano in Iceland.
2010 • Comment • Like

Travelers What!? What volcano?
2010 • Like

Europe Eyjafjallajökull.
2010 • Like

Travelers Uh... gesundheit?
2010 • Like

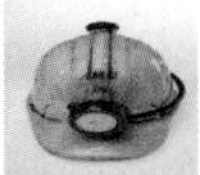

Chilean Miners Well then. This really puts the phrase "getting shafted" in a new light.
2010 • Comment • Like

Chilean Miners Er, actually, no light. Flashlights went dead.
2010 • Like

Chile Woo hoo!

Miners Rescued After 69 Days Trapped Underground
World Rejoices, Mining Company Reports Anus Unpuckering

2010 • Comment • Like

Human Spirit This is a triumph!
2010 • Like

Teamwork This is a great day!
2010 • Like

Hollywood This is GOLD.
2010 • Like

Japan is now in a relationship with **The Pacific Ocean**.
March 15, 2011 • Comment • Like

Japan ...and it's an abusive relationship.
March 15, 2011 • Like

Tectonic Plates Sorry! Again.
March 15, 2011 • Like

Fukushima Nuclear Power Plant OH NO.
March 15, 2011 • Like

Osama Bin Laden Pizza delivery? I didn't order any pizza...
May 1, 2011 • Comment • Like

Seal Team Six likes this.

Satan > Osama Bin Laden HEYOOOO, big man in da house! Welcome, dude! We got a lot of work ahead of us, so let's make sure you're well fed and resteSIKE this is hell you will eat ash and drink my piss. Aloha, bitch.

May 1, 2011 • Comment • Like

Satan PS don't forget: you gotta make 18 hours worth of calls to Time Warner Cable, so maybe skip lunch?

May 1, 2011 • Like

Satan PPS No, the Vuvuzelas never stop. #Imjustthatgood

May 1, 2011 • Like

The Age of Folly

By the beginning of the twenty-first century, humankind was connected itself via technology in ways previous generations would never believe. Smartphones allowed us to immediately witness global events with unprecedented speed and realism. Taking a poo was no longer quiet Me Time, but a front-row seat to distant terrorist attacks, police shootings, or Harlem Shake videos. Fear was on the rise.

Despite this era being the safest, healthiest, most peaceful, and most prosperous age in human history, we began to believe it was all going to hell. So humankind made some bad decisions. We began to deny the changing climate. The United Kingdom decided to leave the European Union, kind of. Not to be outdone, the United States got upset about a woman's email habits and gave the presidency to fellow who struggled with speaking in complete sentences. People declared a state of YOLO.

Culture was changing. Gay marriage was a done deal. Marijuana was legalized. Objective truth became subjective, even though it isn't. People believed the narratives they wanted to be real, rather than the ones that were. Even Facebook underwent a redesign, mostly by Russia. The Age of Folly had arrived.

Costa Concordia
January 19 2012 ·

Shiiiiiiiiiiiiiiiiiiiii

Maritime Insurance and 2k others — 1 Comment

The Poseidon Adventure
amateur

Like · Comment · Share

Autonomous Vehicles checked into **California** and **Nevada.**
January 19 2012 ·

Elon Musk and 34 others — 2 Comments

Professional Drivers
oh no

Obsolesence oh yes I'm afraid

Like · Comment · Share

Friends You May Know

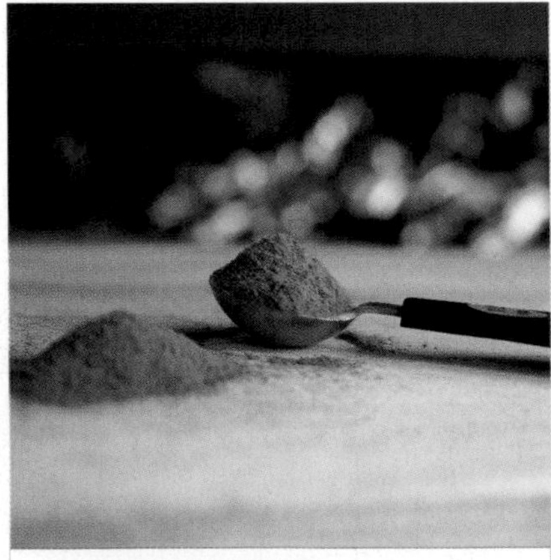

Cinnamon Challenge
Ill-Advised Viral Fad

ADD FRIEND | REMOVE

KONY 2012
Ill-Advised Viral Charity

ADD FRIEND

Planet Earth ▶ Planet Venus

June 9 2012 ·

hellooooooooooooooooooooobyebyeeeeeeeeeeeeeeeeeeeee

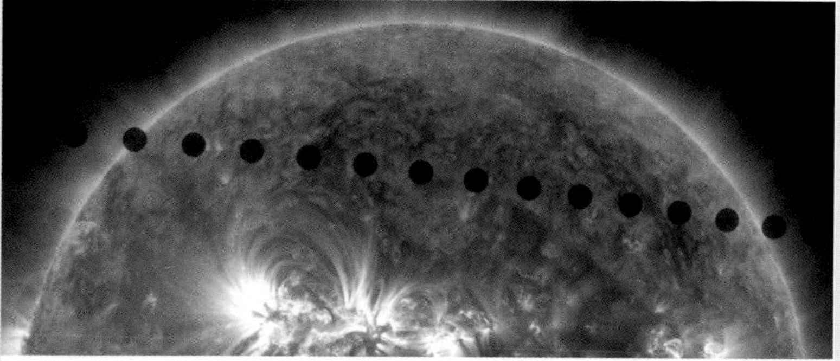

Planet Earth, Planet Mars, and 6 others 2 Comments

Pluto
Why ya'll put "Planet" before your names???

 **Planet Venus** Because we can lol

Like Comment Share

Glaciers

July 4 2012 ·

nah nah naaah nah. hey hey hey. I'm oceannn.

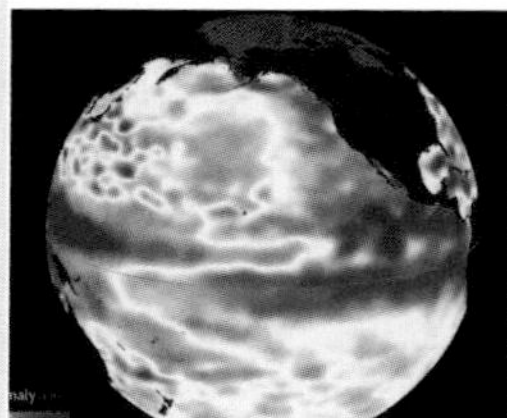

NOAA.COM

2012 Hottest Year on Record

"*Again*" Mutter Scientists

Climate Change and 0 others 3 Comments

T-1000
i know now why you cry

 **Glaciers** melt, but yeah

 **T-1000** 🌊👍🌊

US Supreme Court shared a link.

June 28 2012 ·

BOBLAWSLAWBLOG.COM

Supreme Court Upholds Affordable Care Act, 5-4

Vindication and 150m others 4 Comments

Pres. Barack Obama
A great day. Americans deserve better healthcare.

Sen. Mitch McTurtle
or do they deserve a lengthy Repeal attempt.

Jurisprudence Mitch for god sakes c'mon

Sen. Mitch McTurtle DON'T MITCH ME BITCH

Like Comment Share

Large Hadron Collider

July 4 2012 ·

Delighted to announce the confirmation of the Higgs Boson; the particle of the quantum field that interacts with matter to create the effect of mass.

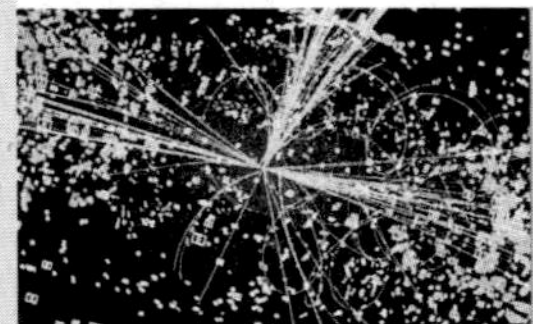

PARTICLEFARTICLE.COM

Higgs Boson FOUND

Still Lost on Normal People

Peter Higgs, Alfred Nobel, and 2m others 3 Comments

Hollywood
Is this that God Particle thing? so it's a particle with god-like powers? or like literal particles of god

Physicists What? Neither. Please read the publication.

Hollywood GOD'S PARTICLES, coming this summer

The Olympics checked into **London**
August 2012 ·

SPORTSYREPORTSY.COM

Summer Games Comes to Country With Little to No Summer

 Abs, Precious Metals, and 50m others 1 Comment

People Watching at Home
100m in 10sec? Pff. Make nachos in a single ad break, then talk

Like Comment Share

Curiosity Rover ▶ Planet Mars ...
August 2012 ·

hello sir may I land upon your face okay great

Beep, Boop, and 100m others 4 Comments

Mars
go for it, I don't have life *OR DO I* hahaha

Curiosity Rover
it is very alone here

NASA Oh you'll be fine!

Opportunity Rover
All work and no play make Jack a dull boy.

Felix Baumgartner checked into **Space**
August 2012 ·

Maaaaaarketttttiiiinnnnnngggg

THEARTOFCORPORATE.COM
Highest Skydive a Success
Sugary Drink Funds Man to New Heights

 Red Bull and 2m others 2 Comments

Coca Cola
ZERO WINGS GIVEN PEOPLE

Like Comment Share

Hurricane Sandy ▶ Humans
October 2012 ·

OCEAN DELIVERY FOR THE EAST COAST, LEAVING IT ON YOUR PORCH

New Jersey and 5 other states 2 Comments

Climate Change
lol but don't worry, not real

Climate Deniers I don't get you, so you must not be!

 Like Comment Share

United States shared a post.
November 6 2012 ·

Glad that's over. Wonder what 2016 will look like?

TWODUDESAGAIN.COM
Barack Obama Defeats Mitt Romney to Win 2nd Term
Sen. Mitch McConnell Furiously Punches Pillow in Office

 Sanity and 330m others — 4 Comments

Voters
More civil, hopefully.

 **Russia** we help next time.

Hillary Clinton
I got an idea #shooin

 **Bernie Sanders** we'll see.

 **The Near Future** HOoo indeed

Like — Comment — Share

Pope Benedict ▶ Cardinal Jorge Bergoglio
February 11 2013 ·

Yo you like hats and robes, right?

 Catholics and 25m others — 2 Comments

Conclave
Your Grace that's not how this works.

 **Pope Benedict** I just want to wear my sweatshorts

Chelyabinsk Meteor
February 15 2013 ·

I CAME IN LIKE A WRECKING BALLLL

 Michael Bay and 4m others — 3 Comments

Earth
okay that one stung.

City of Chelyabinsk
wrecking ball not go 45,000 mph, comrade

Chelyabinsk Glass and Window Repair
I NEVER HIT SO HARD IN LOVE

Like · Comment · Share

City of Boston ▶ Boston Bombers
April 15 2013 ·

HAVAHDYAHD.COM

Attack Unites City Like Never Before; Terrorists Fail to Forsee This Yet Again

 Solidarity and 50 other states — 1 Comments

Boston Police
Whaddya know, we found you. How do ya like dem

Edward Snowden ...
May 2013 ·

Anyone know a house-sitter available now thru... a while?

 Wikileaks, Alex Jones, and 2 others   4 Comments

Edward Snowden
Also a long-term vacation rental, seclusion a plus.

 **Russia** -coughHi-

National Security Agency
Vacation? We have the 'shmurveillance' meeting on Monday tho.

National Security Agency
Dude?

Like   Comment   Share

US Supreme Court shared a link. ...
June 26 2013 ·

5-4, progress wins.

COURTYREPORTY.NET
DOMA STRUCK DOWN
Cranky Religious Folks Despair, Everyone Else Rejoices

 Equality, Love, and 200m others   3 Comments

Justice "Bone-in 'Tonin" Scalia
Booo, gross

Wedding Planning
I'm not as fun as you think...

 **Religious Cake Bakers** Oh this ain't over.

City of Harlem shared a link.
June 26 2013 ·

WE DID NOT INVENT NOR ENDORSE THIS

DOTHEPROCRASTINATE.COM
Harlem Shake Sweeps Nation
Dance Video Consumes Office Productivity Worth Billions

 Costumes, Masks, Props and 200m others 1 Comment

Jump Cut
My moment has arrived!

Like Comment Share

Fads You May Know

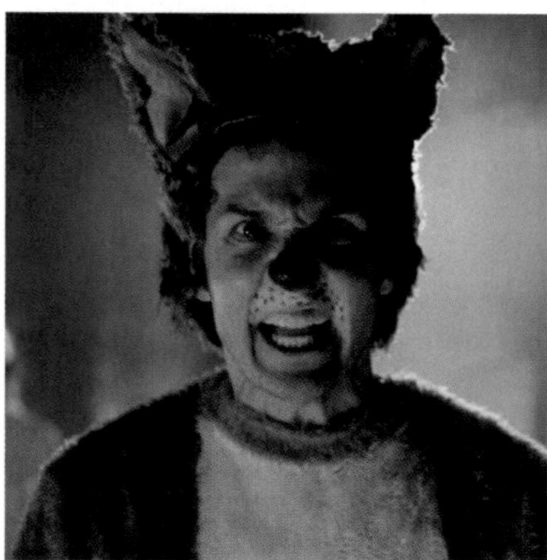

What Does the Fox Say
Hatee-hatee-hatee-ho
ADD FRIEND REMOVE

Screaming Goats
BLWAAAAAAAAH
ADD FRIEND

See All ›

YOLO shared a cliché.
Way Too Much of 2013 ·

President Barack Obama shared a link.
October 1 2013 ·

I am proud and excited to debut the new healthcare service America has been waiting for, Healthcare.gov:

HealthCare.gov

The system is down at the moment.

We are experiencing technical difficulties and hope to have them resolved soon. Please try a

Broke Millennials and 45m others 2 Comments

President Barack Obama
shitballs

Like Comment Share

Iran shared a link.
November 26 2013 ·

FISSIONDECISION.COM
Iran to Cease Nuclear Weapons Development for Sanctions Lift
Let's Hope Nobody Spoils This

Centrifuges and 20m others 2 Comments

President Barack Obama
Achievement Unlocked: Foreign Policy

Fox News
UGH, this does not fit the narrative

Like Comment Share

Legal Marijuana checked into the **State of Colorado.**
Jan 1 2014 · ...

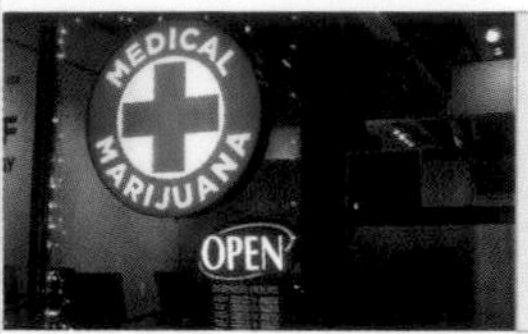

HERBYBLURBY.COM
Marijuana Arrives in Colorado
Boom in Snackfood Innovation Expected

Adult Cartoons, Munchies, and 25m others 2 Comments

State of Colorado
We welcome the Greens.

Religious Conservatives how can u welcome sinful...

Pot Smoker they meant tax dollars, my dudes.

State of Colorado Correct lol WE MINTED BABY

State of Washington oh look a ballot measure of my own!

State of Oregon same lol

Like Comment Share

Ebola
January 2014 · ...

I EXIST TO DO NOTHING BUT PROPAGATE DEATH

Immune Systems and 25m others 2 Comments

Zika
WELCOME BROTHER I DEFORM CHILDREN

World Health Organization
Gonna end you both, you have my word

Center for Disease Control AND MY AXE

Like Comment Share

City of Flint, Michigan
February 2014 ·

Excited to introduce our all-new flavored water: River™
Offering a free trial starting today.

SPITTAKE.COM
Flint Water Available in New Colors 'Taupe Oxide' and 'Burnt Dirt'

 Town Hall Meetings and 5m others 6 Comments

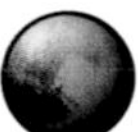

Flint Residents
No thanks, make it stop

City of Flint, Michigan we said free trial, not voluntary

Flint Residents Are you serious, make this stop!

City of Flint, Michigan One moment

Flint Residents What are you waiting for!?

City of Flint, Michigan media spotlight to shift.

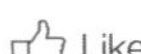

Like Comment Share

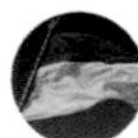

Ukraine ▸ President Yanukovych
February 2014 ·

TFW you order anti-protest laws and get a revolution.

PUNCHABLEFACES.NET
Corrupt Ukrainian President Flees
You Guessed It, to Russia

 Europe and 8m others 2 Comments

Russia
What if army of "separatists" suddenly arrive?
Asking for friend

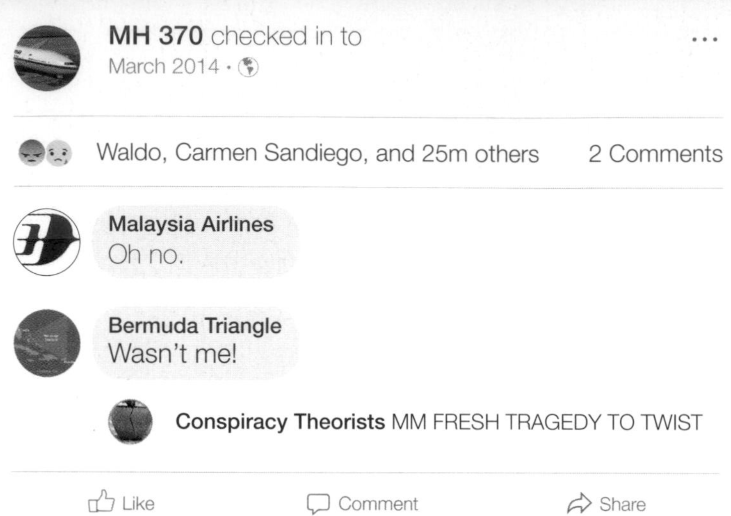

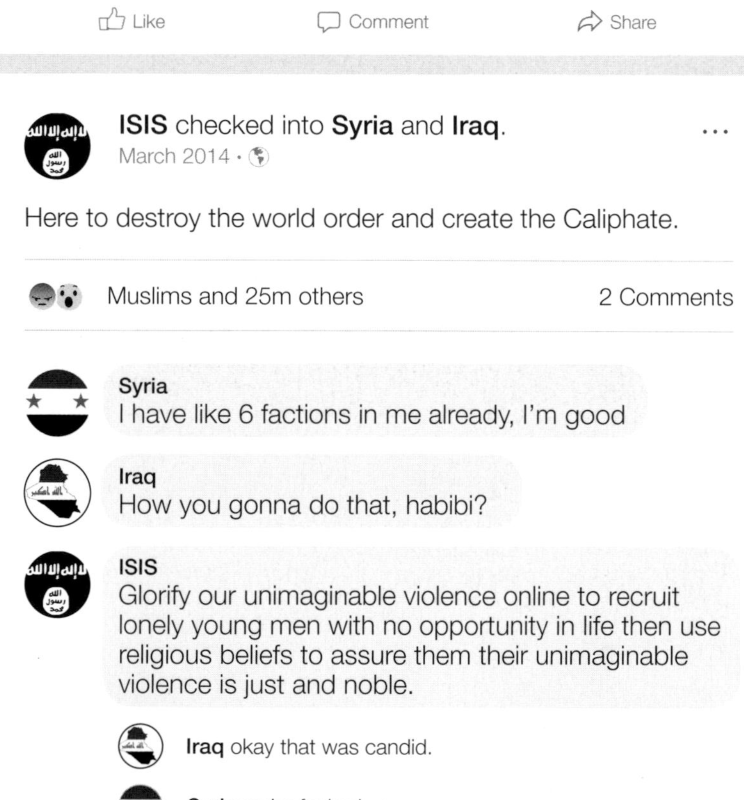

Bashar Al Assad ▶ Syria
March 2014 ·

Just let me dictate you baby shhh stop fighting you'll like it

Ice Bucket Challenge
[gaspgaspgasp]
ADD FRIEND REMOVE

"Let It Go"
Earworm Epidemic
ADD FRIEND R

See All 〉

Ukraine ▶ Russia
July 2014 ·

do you ever stop and wonder, am *I* the villain?

MODERNMEDDLER.COM
Russians Destroy Airliner by Mistake
Definitely Will Say Otherwise

 NATO and 25m others 2 Comments

Russia
West propaganda, comrade. PS no.

 **Netherlands** There will be a full investigation.

 **Russia** ooo, expensive propoganda

Journalists
You keep using that word. I don't think it means what you think it means.

 **Russia** means "fake news" comrade

 **Russia** mm I like this phrase, Fake News. Has nice rin...

 Like  Comment  Share

Russia ▶ Crimea Penninsula
October 2014 ·

Welcome comrade.

 Annexation and 25m others — 2 Comments

Ukraine
what do you mean "welcome"

 **Russia** Crimea come to us, we happy to take

 **Russia** I mean have

 **Ukraine** WHY IS YOUR ARMY HERE

 **Russia** no army, west propaganda

United States
You are disrupting a valid democracy.

 **Russia** just wait lol

Comment

Scotland ▶ United Kingdom
September 2014 ·

Having a wee vote tae see if we inty ye, or oot!

 Freeeeeedooooom and 25m others — 2 Comments

David Cameron
I beg your pardon?

 **Wales** "to see if we're in or out"

 **David Cameron** oh. OH

United Kingdom
calm down nobody's leavin' anyone m8

 **The Near Future** not yet lol

Hong Kong
September 2014 ·

~~FREE ELECTIONS NOW~~

Xi Jinping and 3m others 2 Comments

Chinese Communist Party
😏

Like Comment Share

Rosetta Spacecraft ▶ Comet 67P/C-G
December 2014 ·

From Tuesday's shoot, OMG you look STUNNING

Ice, Dust, Gravity, and 25m others 2 Comments

Comet 67P/C-G:
:-O omg I had no I was off-gassing that much lol! So embarrassing! Will you take one more?

Rosetta Spacecraft babe I'm taking like 100,000 more

Hillary Clinton checked in to the **US Presidential Race**

April 2015 ·

#shocker

GLASSCEILINGSHMASSSHMEILING.COM

Our Next President Is a Woman

Probably.

Democrats and 25m others 2 Comments

Jeb Bush
See you next November!

The Near Future oh Jeb!..

Like Comment Share

India Plate ▶ Eurasian Plate

April 2015 ·

Aaaah, that's better.

Kinetic Energy and 3m others 2 Comments

Nepal
STOP STOP STOP STOP

Like Comment Share

Bruce Jenner checked in to **Caitlyn Jenner**

April 2015 ·

Aaaah, that's better.

Daytime Television and 25m others 2 Comments

Personal Pronouns
fml

Donald Trump checked in to the **Republican Primary**
June 2015 ·

Hubris and 3m others 2 Comments

Democrats
lol well he'll be amusing!

The Near Future Yeah. Well.

Cuba is friends with the **United States.**
July 2015 ·

Common Decency and 20m others 2 Comments

Cigar Aficcionados
Oh. my god.

Baseball Scouts SWEET JESUS

Comment

Refugees checked in to **Europe**.
June 2015 ·

We PROMISE we are not here to take your jobs, we're here because our jobs were taken by air strikes.

YOUWOULDTOO.COM
Millions Flee Middle East Conflicts
Many Seek "Ability To Stay Alive"

Empathy and 20m others 2 Comments

Scared Old People
Turn them away! they steal our jobs

Automation lol, bro...

New Horizons shared a photo.
July 2015 ·

European Space Agency and 3m others 2 Comments

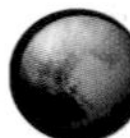

Pluto
OMG my first friend!!!!!

Pluto
wait where are you going--

Like Comment Share

Flagpoles ▶ The Confederate Flag
July 2015 ·

Look, it's... not working out.

Racism
MY HORCRUX--!

Like Comment Share

SpaceX Falcon 9
December 2015 ·

WHOA THIS FEELS VERY UNNATURAL

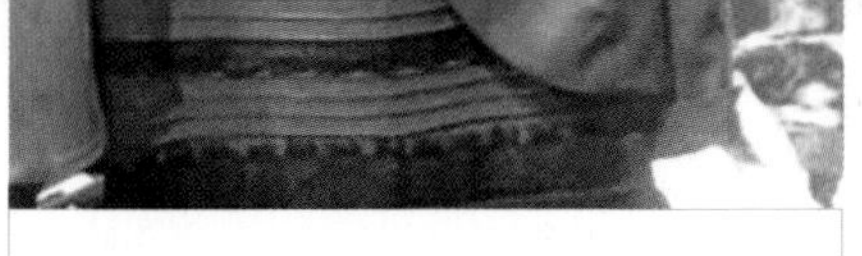

Black and Blue Dress
Laurel

ADD FRIEND | REMOVE

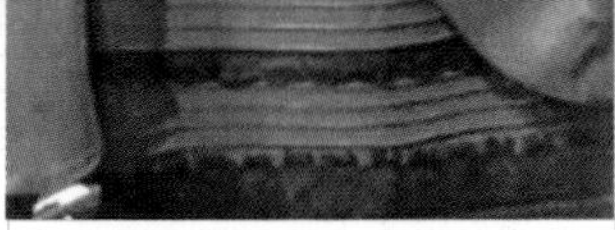

White and Gold Dress
Yanny

ADD FRIEND | R

See All 〉

Women checked into **US Army Rangers** ...
December 2015 ·

PRACTICALTACTICALFAN.COM
First Women Become Army Rangers
Insecure Men Take Offense

Equality and 28 others — 2 Comments

The Pentagon
You'll do fine on the front lines.

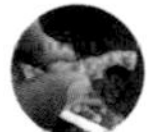

Internet Trolls
TO THE KEYBOARDS, BOYS

Like — Comment — Share

Paris Climate Accord ...
December 2015 ·

124 countries will defeat this global threat together.

Earth, Life, Civilization, and 7 billion others — 3 Comments

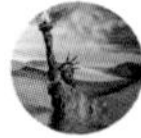

The Apocalypse
ugh that was going so wellllll

Coal and Oil Industry
😫😫

Sen. Mitch McTurtle Don't worry babe I'll make this ri...

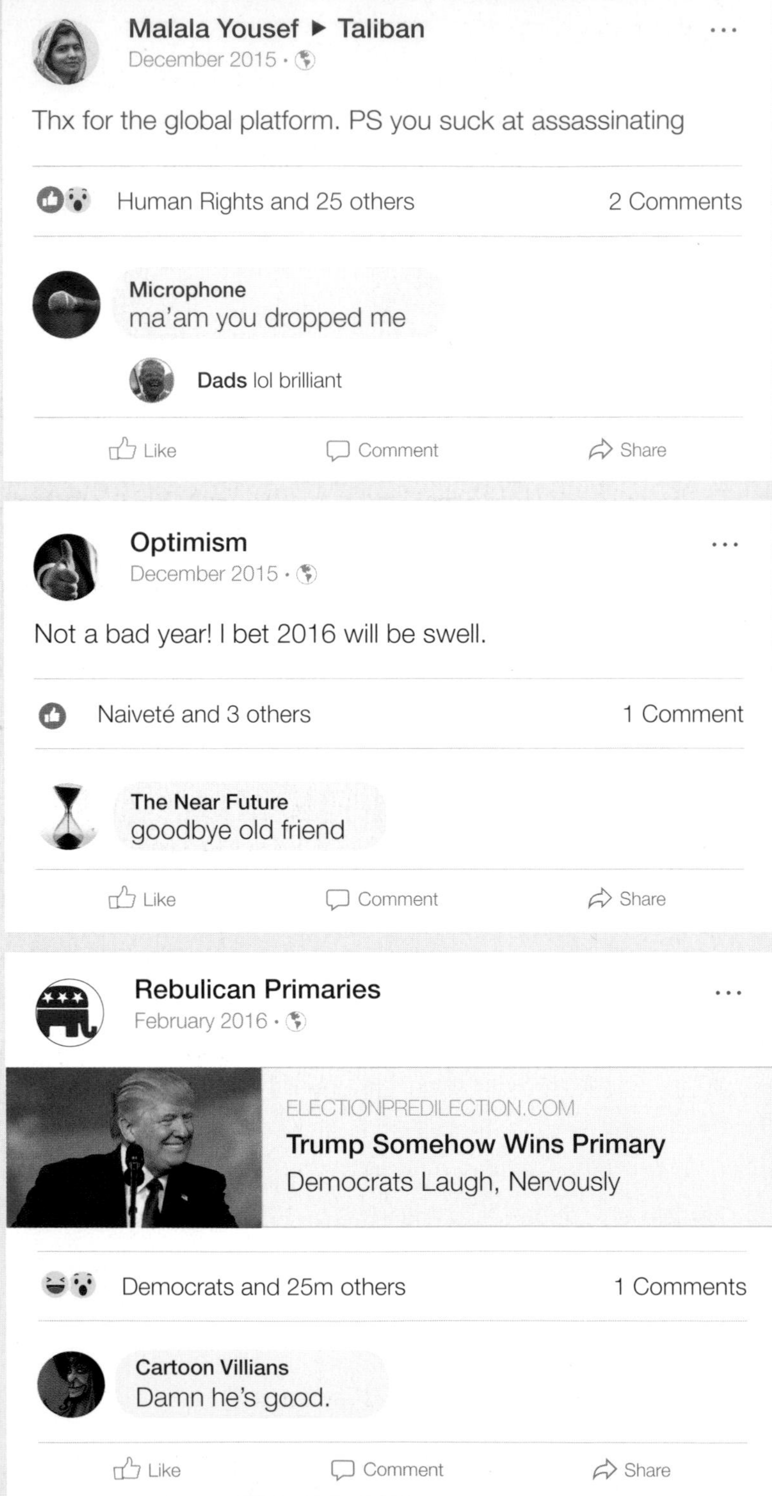

Malala Yousef ▶ Taliban
December 2015 ·

Thx for the global platform. PS you suck at assassinating

Human Rights and 25 others — 2 Comments

Microphone ma'am you dropped me

Dads lol brilliant

Like · Comment · Share

Optimism
December 2015 ·

Not a bad year! I bet 2016 will be swell.

Naiveté and 3 others — 1 Comment

The Near Future goodbye old friend

Like · Comment · Share

Rebulican Primaries
February 2016 ·

ELECTIONPREDILECTION.COM
Trump Somehow Wins Primary
Democrats Laugh, Nervously

Democrats and 25m others — 1 Comments

Cartoon Villians Damn he's good.

Like · Comment · Share

President Barack Obama
March 16 2016 ·

Happy to nominate Merrick Garland for the Supreme Court, I look forward to his confirmation hearing in the Senate.

Due Process and 300m others 2 Comments

Senator Mitch McTurtle
what hearing

President Barack Obama According to the rules of govern...

Senator Mitch McTurtle WHAT RULES

The Joker HAHAHAH I too like to watch the world burn

Like Comment Share

Mass Shootings checked in to **Baton Rouge.**
July 2016 ·

Like Comment Share

Mass Shootings checked in to **Cascade Mall.**
September 2016 ·

Like Comment Share

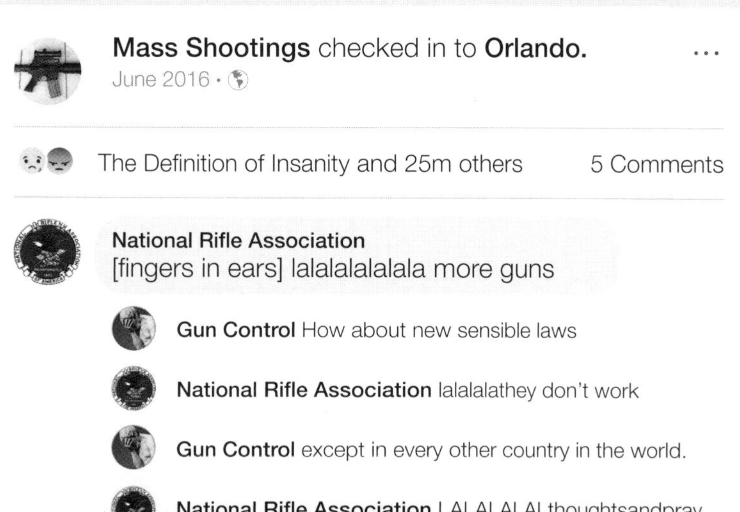

Mass Shootings checked in to **Orlando.**
June 2016 ·

The Definition of Insanity and 25m others 5 Comments

National Rifle Association
[fingers in ears] lalalalalalala more guns

Gun Control How about new sensible laws

National Rifle Association lalalalathey don't work

Gun Control except in every other country in the world.

National Rifle Association LALALALALthoughtsandpray...

"Brexit" Vote checked in to the **United Kingdom**
June 2016 · 🌎

Vote Leave so you can blame your shit life on others.

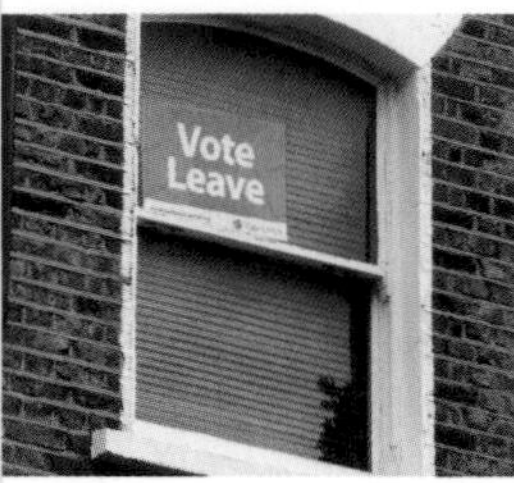

LEANINTOTHEISLANDTHING.COM
UK Holds Vote to Leave EU
Scared Old People and Racists Attempt to Impart Economic Self-Ruin

Russia and 25m others — 4 Comments

David Cameron
No chance.

Europe Awkward.

United States
lolol well you win 2016's democracy fuck-up award

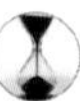

The Near Future year ain't over bud

Like Comment Share

Believe (Verb) ▶ Donald Trump
July 2016 · 🌎

FWIW the more you use me the less impact I have.

Confirmation Bias and 25m others — 3 Comments

Tremendous (Adj.)
Tried having this talk, no luck.

Trump Supporters
FALSE

Fox News
@TheDonald I got u fam

 Like  Comment Share

Wildfire ▶ State of California
September 2016 ·

If only there was a phenomena like water falling from the skies lol

 Drought, Wind, and 4 others — 1 Comment

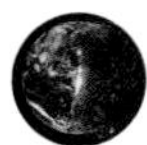

Climate Change
Some of my fave work tbh. glaciers r booriiiing

 Like  Comment  Share

Election Day checked in to **United States**
September 2016 ·

THERECANONLYBEONE.ORG

Americans Head to the Polls

Hillary Clinton v. Donald Trump: Voters Cast Ballots for President

 Russia and 25m others — 19 Comments

Democrats
You mean Madam President lol

The Near Future
Well, the moment has arrived.

 **Democrats** she making history, amirite lol

 **The Near Future** No you are not.

Hillary Clinton
What's happening...

Democrats
wha-- wait

Republicans
wait-- wha?

Television Pundits

Pollsters

Democrats

Republicans

Democrats

Europe

Vladimir Putin

Barack Obama

Bernie Supporters

Protest Sign Supply Co.

Hillary Clinton
What just happened?

Simon & Schuster how do you feel about losing the 'just'

Satan
Is this why its snowing?!?!

Like Comment Share

Chicago Cubs
November 2016 ·

World Series Champions!

Babe Ruth, Curses, and 50m others 2 Comments

Satan
lol oh THIS is why

Police Brutality checked in to **United States**
November 2016 ·

ETTUBRUTALITY.ORG
Protests Against Police Violence Erupt; Turns Out Cops Can Be Pretty Bad

 Justice and 4 others — 1 Comment

Black Lives Matter
Got you on camera now.

 **All Lives Matter** okay but MEEEEEEEE

 Comment 

The Year 2016 ▶ Death
December 2016 ·

Go easy on the beloved celebrities please, I've been a rough one already.

 Tributes and 15m others — 4 Comment

Prince
💀

David Bowie
💀

Alan Rickman
💀

Carrie Fisher
💀

The Year 2016
dude

  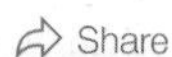

Donald Trump checked in to the **White House**

January 2017 ·

Too Many Americans 2 Comments

Reality
@Democrats yes this is me right now, stop asking.

Hillary Clinton
How's this for putting on a good face.

Melania Trump same

Steve Bannon
Proud of my boy.

Vladimir Putin same

Nature's Portents
A cold, quiet rain as the speech begins feels right.

Like Comment Share

North Korea checked in to **Space**

April 2015 ·

Brinksmanship and 25m others 3 Comments

Donald Trump
Tensions are high, but let us redouble our efforts to restore he bonds of friendship and a peaceful future.

Americans wow, was-- did you actually say that?

Donald Trump no I said "I have a bigger nuke button!"

Humans ▶ Moon
August 2017 ·

whoooaaaaa

ALLTHEWAY-ACROSSTHESKY.NET
Total Solar Eclipse Across the US
Everyone Stop Fighting and Look Up

 Shadows and 25m others — 2 Comments

Earth
shoulda seen it when u guys had no idea what was happening lol... shit your loincloths

NASA
PSA: remember to not look at the sun directly.

 **Flat Earther** why, what are you trying to hide!

 **NASA** Your eyeballs, from your brain.

 **Flat Earther** LIES, SCIENCE HIGH PRIEST

 Like — Comment —  Share

Alyssa Milano shared a post ...
October 2017 ·

If all the women who have been sexually harassed or assaulted wrote "Me too." as a status, we might give people a sense of the magnitude of the problem.

 Women You Know and 163m others — 2 Comments

The Patriarchy
What problem baby

 **Retribution** we haven't met but we're about to big style

 Like — Comment — Share

Elon's Roadster ▶ Elon Musk
January 2018 ·

ooo what's this fancy new garage about?

Elon Musk, ΔV, and 25m others 2 Comments

Elon's Roadster
AHHHHHHHHHHHHHHH

Space hey little guy

Like Comment Share

Mass Shootings checked in to **Parkland High School**
February 2018 ·

The Definition of Insanity and 750k others 2 Comments

Students
#walkout

National Rifle Association
hmm, long walks vs. buying congresspeople with campaign donations...lol enjoy your stroll

Students
Oh look, I turn 18 before Election Day.

Like Comment Share

Prince Harry and **Megan Marhkle**
May 2018 ·

Got Married

May 19, 2018

 Wuv, Twue Wuv, Mawwige, and 25m others 2 Comments

United Kingdom
I love my fam.

United States I GET IT NOW

Like Comment Share

Donald Trump shared a post
June 2018 ·

DIY-SHITTYIDEAS.ORG
How to Separate Immigrant Children from Parents and Accomplish Nothing

 Decency and 25m others 2 Comments

Statue of Liberty
"Give us your tired, your weary..." Any bells?

Trump Supporters
I will find a way to defend this I just need a sec

Like Comment Share

Hawaii shared a post
June 2018 ·

excuse me sorry pardon me comin thru gangway red hot

Conclusion

And now we find ourselves at the end.

I wish it weren't, dear reader. I wish we could carry on forever, with the end seemingly close but never actually arriving. I'm not Peter Jackson though, and books are inherently finite objects.

History, however, continues. Time drags it along, like a mother with her child at the supermarket. A thousand years in the future, people will be able to read about the amazing things that have happened since now. They'll read about the tragedies and triumphs that we have yet to know. They'll read about the heroes and villains, the pariahs and iconoclasts, the superstars and legends, all of whom have yet to be born. Then they'll upload their emotion-states to the nexus and mind-shift to work on exo-planet B7, owned by Exxon Facebogoogle.

Yes, a thousand years from we will have a new epoch of history to satirize on a News Feed. Who knows, maybe then I'll write a follow-up. I'll run it by my publisher.

Finally, we should keep our fingers crossed that we as a species learn to coexist peacefully. Despite our many differences, we have much more in common—something we seem to willfully ignore. Let us hope that we look after our little rock as it hurtles around the sun, for it is the only oasis we have in the cold dark void of space. And let us hope our tendency for belligerence fades, and that world leaders take their fingers off their respective Red Buttons; otherwise we may succeed in eliminating ourselves.

I will leave you now, dear reader, as my friend Brandon is telling me we're up next on the pool table, and that it's my round at the bar, so put away the laptop, dickface, he'll take a beer, nothing too dark but not too light, and maybe some jalapeno poppers if they have them, or onion rings, or whatever, just something fried because he didn't eat lunch today and he's got to drive at some point.

Fare thee well, reader, and thank you for reading. Your purchase helped me subsidize Brandon's beer. And jalapeno poppers. If they have them.